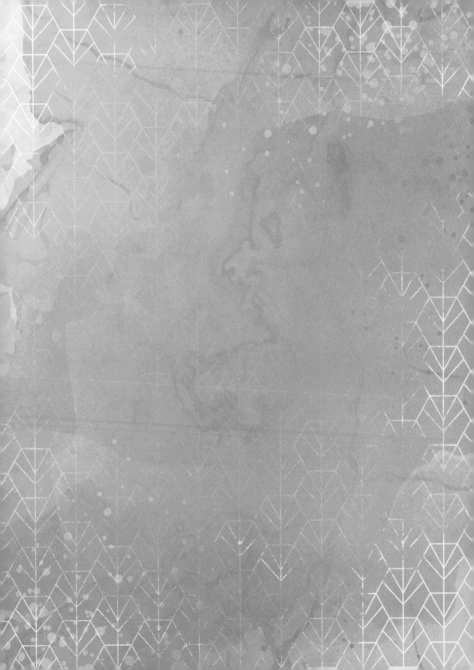

LET FAITH RISE UP

LET FAITH RISE UP

Devotions & Prayers for Women

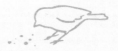

Carey Scott

BARBOUR
PUBLISHING

Cover Design: Greg Jackson, Thinkpen Design

Published by Barbour Publishing, Inc., 1810 Barbour Drive, Uhrichsville, Ohio 44683, www.barbourbooks.com

Our mission is to inspire the world with the life-changing message of the Bible.

 Member of the
Evangelical Christian
Publishers Association

Printed in China

You're Invited to a Grand Adventure!

Every day you get to choose how you'll respond to life's challenges. Will you stand firm as you trust God, or will you crumble under the weight and pressure of life's difficulties? Will you cling to His promises to save, heal, and restore, or will fear win out?

God is inviting you to a grand adventure with Him, and faith is your ticket! Rise up, beautiful one, and embrace all He has planned for you. And never forget you were created *on* purpose and *for* a purpose.

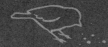

Faith Pleases God

It's impossible to please God apart from faith. And why? Because anyone who wants to approach God must believe both that he exists and that he cares enough to respond to those who seek him.

HEBREWS 11:6 MSG

Your faith pleases God. Every time you choose to trust Him rather than sit in fear and worry, He notices. When you believe Him for a miracle, He's delighted. God knows you have the free will to choose what you do or do not rely on, so choosing faith over all else speaks volumes. And it's with that kind of confidence you can ask the Lord for what you need.

Do you want more wisdom or discernment? Are you looking for peace or joy? Maybe you desire a godly perspective on a worldly fear. Are you needing comfort? Hope? Perseverance? Do you long for reassurance of your value as a woman? Need help trusting again? Or maybe you could use strength for the rocky road you're traveling on right now. Whatever it may be, know deep in your heart that God is real, and He really cares for you.

Father, grow my faith in You so there is no doubt of Your sovereignty. Keep close as I walk through both the good and hard times. I believe in You with all my heart, and I know You love me! Let that truth be what drives me to You when I am in need. In Jesus' name I pray. Amen.

Faith versus Doubt

So Jesus answered and said to them, "Assuredly, I say to you,
if you have faith and do not doubt, you will not only do what
was done to the fig tree, but also if you say to this mountain, 'Be
removed and be cast into the sea,' it will be done. And what-
ever things you ask in prayer, believing, you will receive."

MATTHEW 21:21–22 NKJV

Doubt has a way of ruining everything faith inspires. It causes you to hesitate rather than believe. It sows uncertainty into your spirit, so you never find peace. Doubt creates a reservoir of reservation, ensuring you never run out of skepticism. Even more, it keeps you from enjoying the gift of confidence that comes from anchoring your faith in God. There is power in your faith.

But choosing to believe God *can* and *will* unlocks possibility. It grows hope. It allows you to live with an expectancy that makes you giddy. And you will find a level of optimism you may have never had. Your decision to trust God will empower you to live with a beautiful boldness as you believe the Lord will show up in meaningful ways.

Father, I confess my doubt and ask You to grow my
faith so I can enjoy You more. Deepen my trust in Your
ability. And make me fearless because of my belief in
Your goodness. In Jesus' name I pray. Amen.

The Gift of Listening

*The point is: Before you trust, you have to listen. But unless
Christ's Word is preached, there's nothing to listen to.*

ROMANS 10:17 MSG

Think about it. You became a believer because you heard someone share
the Gospel. You heard them talk about how Jesus intersected with their
life—how He showed up at the perfect time. Their enthusiasm was
contagious, and it inspired you to dig deeper into what a relationship with
Jesus looked like. In time, you realized the power of faith and embraced
it as your own.

Let your ears always be trained on the good news of Christ. Not
only is it a faith-grower for you, but it will help others find hope too.
There's no substitute for His message. The truth is, a million other voices
are fighting for your attention. This world is a loud place. But when you
hear the Word of God and the testimony of the faithful, you'll realize
everything else is just noise.

Father, train my ears to listen only for Your still, small voice.
The world is loud, but I want to hear You above all else. Keep my
heart pointed in Your direction and my attention on You. Comfort
me with Your Word. And help me stay focused in my faith and
filled with hope as I grow in You. In Jesus' name I pray. Amen.

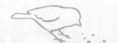

9

A Leap of Faith

What is faith? It is the confident assurance that something we want is going to happen. It is the certainty that what we hope for is waiting for us, even though we cannot see it up ahead.

HEBREWS 11:1 TLB

Faith isn't always easy to have. They don't call it a *leap* for nothing, amen? And while we may say we fully trust God to be present in our difficult situations, sometimes we battle with feelings of doubt. But the Word is clear when it says faith means confident assurance of the Lord's hand in your situation. It's a firm certainty that what you hope for will come to pass, even though you're unable to see into the future. It's steadfastness in your belief that God will intervene at the right time and in the right way. Faith is conviction.

Think about what faith looks like in your life right now in light of the struggles you're facing. Do you believe God is in control and will see you through to the other side? Do you have confidence everything will work out just as He has planned? Take the leap and know you can entrust the outcome to Him.

Father, You know how hard it is for me to give up control. It's something I've struggled with for a long time. But I'm going to take a leap of faith and trust You with my circumstances. In Jesus' name I pray. Amen.

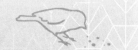

Asking with the Right Heart

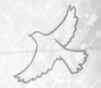

*So Jesus answered and said to them, "Have faith in God. For
assuredly, I say to you, whoever says to this mountain, 'Be removed
and be cast into the sea,' and does not doubt in his heart, but believes
that those things he says will be done, he will have whatever he
says. Therefore I say to you, whatever things you ask when you
pray, believe that you receive them, and you will have them."*

MARK 11:22–24 NKJV

Sometimes people read today's passage thinking it means God is a genie in a bottle. They believe they can ask for money, cars, fame. . .and whatever they ask for will be granted. But what we have to understand is that our heart is to be aligned with His so that anything we ask will match up with His desires.

You may need provision to pay bills, not take a lavish vacation. You may want your book to sell many copies so His name will be glorified, not your own. You might need a car because yours broke down versus wanting to keep up with the Joneses. Ask with the right heart and watch what happens.

**Father, give me the courage and faith to ask for the
things I need. I know You care! Even more, align my heart
with Yours so I ask for the right things. Help me trust
You for provision! In Jesus' name I pray. Amen.**

Never Earned

For by grace you have been saved by faith. Nothing you did
could ever earn this salvation, for it was the love gift from God
that brought us to Christ! So no one will ever be able to boast,
for salvation is never a reward for good works or human striving.

EPHESIANS 2:8–9 TPT

What a huge relief to know our salvation isn't dependent on our actions. If that were true, heaven's population would be zero. Right? To realize eternity is secured by faith alone allows a collective sigh as we thank the Lord for making a way for us to be with Him forever. God knew if we had to earn our salvation, it would be impossible for us to achieve.

Jesus' death on the cross paid the price for your sins—past, present, future. When you receive this gift, believing Jesus is the Son of God who died and rose again to wash you clean in the eyes of God the Father, that faith saves you. Give Him the glory and take none for yourself. Oh how He loves you.

Father, thank You for not requiring me to earn my salvation.
That would be a disaster! And thanks for making a way for
me to spend eternity in heaven with You! I receive the gift of
Jesus and His complete work on the cross, and I am grateful
to be called a child of God. In Jesus' name I pray. Amen.

Faith in Action

Do I hear you professing to believe in the one and only God, but then observe you complacently sitting back as if you had done something wonderful? That's just great. Demons do that, but what good does it do them? Use your heads! Do you suppose for a minute that you can cut faith and works in two and not end up with a corpse on your hands?

JAMES 2:19–20 MSG

While good works won't earn you a place in heaven, they do demonstrate a heart for God. When you receive Jesus as your Savior, let the joy of your salvation be a powerful catalyst to make changes in your life. Desire to be more like Him, intentional to live a life of faith that points to God in heaven. Spend time in the Word, time with other believers, and time in prayer and worship. Simply put, allow your faith and actions to be in a harmonious relationship.

If you've accepted Jesus but have no desire to connect with Him, let that be a red flag. If you have no stirring in your heart to live differently, be questioning if you truly made the decision to become a follower. Faith in action is evidence of a relationship with the Lord. Ask Him to help you want to know Him deeply and seek Him with all your heart.

Father, help me be a woman who genuinely pursues my faith and all that goes with it. In Jesus' name I pray. Amen.

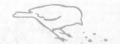

Don't Figure It Out on Your Own

Trust GOD from the bottom of your heart; don't try to figure out everything on your own. Listen for GOD's voice in everything you do, everywhere you go; he's the one who will keep you on track.

PROVERBS 3:5–6 MSG

If we're going to be women of faith, then we have to surrender our need to figure everything out ourselves. Truth is, we come by it honestly. We come from a long line of women who have managed homes and families, businesses and careers, and we've learned to be proactive in our success. We watched those before us work hard and handle whatever came their way. And while their example can be a powerful blessing to pass along, it backfires when we choose to trust ourselves over God.

Having faith means looking to the Lord for answers. It means leaning on Him for direction. Rather than determining your own way, you choose to listen for His voice telling you the next step. God is the One who will guide your steps so you can stay on the right path. Trust Him from the bottom of your heart.

Father, I'm grateful for the women who came before me because they modeled what a strong, capable woman looks like. But I know my strength and wisdom come from You alone. You're the One who will keep me on track. Train my ears to listen for Your voice over the voices of others. In Jesus' name I pray. Amen.

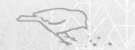

The God of Possible

"Not one promise from God is empty of power.
Nothing is impossible with God!"

LUKE 1:37 TPT

There's nothing God cannot do in your life and the lives of those you love. Are you needing a medical miracle? Are you struggling to find significance after your divorce? Do you crave a community of friends? Is your child heading in the wrong direction? Does your friend need an emotional breakthrough? Are you lacking basic necessities? Has grief overtaken you? Are you having trouble getting pregnant or have you suffered another miscarriage? Friend, place your impossibilities at the feet of God and talk to Him about your battle with hopelessness.

Ask the Lord to grow your faith. Let Him be the One who opens your eyes to new possibilities. Not only can God do it, but when you trust Him for it, He will do it! Remember, He knows what you need even before you do. His timing is perfect and punctual. God is unlimited and unbound. And because He loves you and always has your best interests in mind, His promises will be fulfilled. Take it to the bank.

Father, I love knowing nothing is impossible with You. That truth allows me to dream big and hope bigger. It keeps me from falling into the pit of despair. And I fully believe You will bring forth the right opportunities at the right time. I trust You. In Jesus' name I pray. Amen.

Focus on Faith

The path we walk is charted by faith, not by what we see with our eyes.

2 Corinthians 5:7 VOICE

If we focus on the struggles we are facing, we're going to end up discouraged and disappointed. They will quickly beat us down and leave us in despair. Life is full of heartache and always will be. But we can find peace and joy regardless of the hard seasons by activating our faith in the Lord. We can live in freedom by placing every chain that threatens to bind us at His feet. We can choose to believe what God says over what our circumstances feel like. Living by faith is a choice, and one we must make every day.

Think about the situations causing stress and strife right now. Are you focusing on God or the scary circumstances instead? Ask yourself if you're at peace or full of fear. Do you have more moments of joy or tears? For faith to rise up, spend time today sharing your heart with the Lord. Confess your struggle with trust. And ask God to train your eyes to focus on faith above everything else.

Father, help me focus on You and Your promises. Let me
stand strong rather than cower in hopelessness. Too often
I let my circumstances dictate my mood, but no more.
Grow my faith so I can stay hopeful, trusting You are in
control and I am safe. In Jesus' name I pray. Amen.

Nothing Trumps God's Wisdom

And my speech and my preaching were not with persuasive words of human wisdom, but in demonstration of the Spirit and of power, that your faith should not be in the wisdom of men but in the power of God.

1 CORINTHIANS 2:4–5 NKJV

Today's verse is a great reminder from Paul to be intentional about where we anchor our faith. Too often we're swayed by wise words from the world. We rely on finding time-tested solutions to replicate in our own situations. We look to those who have gone before us and follow their prescribed ten-step program for success. And while others may offer good and wholesome ideas, God's wisdom won't be trumped.

There's nothing wrong with seeking advice from others. Many well-meaning people are ready to offer their suggestions. Maybe you have a mentor who loves Jesus and speaks truth. Talking to a pastor or friend or reading a book by your favorite Christian author can refocus you and bring encouragement. But where you must be careful is ensuring you don't allow anything or anyone to override your faith in the Lord's knowledge. He is the supreme source!

Father, help me trust You above all else. When I get advice from others, remind me to seek Your endorsement. I can look in Your Word for confirmation. I can pray, asking for validation. But keep me focused on Your wisdom alone. I know I can always trust it! In Jesus' name I pray. Amen.

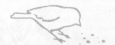

For God So Loved You

For God expressed His love for the world in this way: He gave
His only Son so that whoever believes in Him will not face
everlasting destruction, but will have everlasting life.

JOHN 3:16 VOICE

You may have read this verse a million times, but let it fall fresh on you right now. This is the verse we hang our faith on because it demonstrates God's passionate and unwavering love for us. Can you even imagine such a sacrifice? But this is how we know the Lord is Someone we can trust with anything and everything. To allow His only Son to die so we'd no longer be separated from Him because of sin is almost unbelievable. It's something we can't imagine doing in our own life. But this is how God expressed His love for us.

What keeps you from trusting the Lord? What are the barriers that block your faith? Spend time today with Him and ask for revelation. Ask for God to break down the walls of unbelief. Let Him into those painful places so you can be healed. Unpack your fears and insecurities with your Father. What a beautiful way to let your faith rise up so you can walk it out with confidence.

Father, thank You for Jesus. Thank You that because of
His death, I have life. Grow my faith so I am mighty in
You. I surrender all. In Jesus' name I pray. Amen.

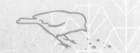

Blind Faith

*By faith Abraham obeyed when he was called to go out to
the place which he would receive as an inheritance. And
he went out, not knowing where he was going.*

HEBREWS 11:8 NKJV

There are times God asks us to obey and we've no idea where our *yes*
will take us. We aren't sure how we will get from here to there. We feel
completely unqualified. We wonder if God is crazy for thinking we could
do what is asked. It may feel so far out of our comfort zone we want to
hide. We may think our past seasons of sinning disqualify us and our
current bad choices don't help. When we look at our busy life, we may
not see how what God is asking will work. But the truth is, we can trust
an unknown future to a known God.

Your job is to listen and obey. It's to trust that if God is calling you
to something, He'll work out every detail along the way. It's believing
that His will and ways are loftier than yours. And it requires a steadfast
faith that God will give you everything you need if you ask. So before
you shake your head and say no, why not instead bow your head and say,
"Yes, Lord. Send me"?

**Father, give me the courage and confidence to follow
Your lead. Help my faith grow deeper so I trust You
no matter what. In Jesus' name I pray. Amen.**

The God of Details

By faith they passed through the Red Sea as by dry land,
whereas the Egyptians, attempting to do so, were drowned.

HEBREWS 11:29 NKJV

As the Israelites stood with the Egyptian army behind them and the Red Sea before them, imagine the fear they must have felt. God, through Moses, had delivered them from slavery, certainly growing their faith tenfold. But as they wondered in that moment if they would live or die, do you think they began to question God? Do you think their faith began to waver? In the end, not only did the Lord part the sea and allow His children to escape the Egyptian army, but He also dried the ocean floor so they crossed on dry land.

You can have faith that God is in the details. Trust Him, even when you feel surrounded on every side by the enemy. When your circumstances look hopeless, watch the Lord shine. Not only will He prove faithful in the big stuff, but you can have faith God will also be in the fine points. He will part the sea for you and even clear it of mud. That's the kind of God you serve.

Father, I didn't realize how detailed You are, but I see it now. Thank You for promising to intervene in every aspect of the issues I face—even the ones I may not be aware of. I appreciate Your faithfulness to take care of me! In Jesus' name I pray. Amen.

Cheered On from Heaven

As for us, we have all of these great witnesses who encircle us like clouds. So we must let go of every wound that has pierced us and the sin we so easily fall into. Then we will be able to run life's marathon race with passion and determination, for the path has been already marked out before us.

HEBREWS 12:1 TPT

You have an audience in the heavenlies that is cheering you on. They encircle you, watching as you live out your faith. Be encouraged knowing you're not alone in the battles you face. Many are rooting for your victory!

Let the knowledge of this audience be what inspires you to live in freedom from your hurts and hang-ups. Holding on to them only prolongs the pain and keeps you in bondage. You refuse to forgive. You play the offenses on repeat in your mind. You plot revenge. You keep anger alive. And you sacrifice peace, purpose, and passion in the process. Because of your faith, choose to run life's marathon with your eyes and heart on God. And when life feels heavy, imagine the cheers of the celestial audience encompassing you.

Father, I'm encouraged to know I'm not alone in the battles. To think I have You and a cheering section makes me smile. May this fresh awareness infuse my faith so I can run this race well and inspire as many as I can along the way. In Jesus' name I pray. Amen.

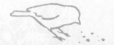

Embracing His Correction

Fully embrace God's correction as part of your training, for he is doing what any loving father does for his children. For who has ever heard of a child who never had to be corrected? We all should welcome God's discipline as the validation of authentic sonship. For if we have never once endured his correction it only proves we are strangers and not sons.

HEBREWS 12:7–8 TPT

No one likes to be corrected. Being reprimanded for stepping out of line is never a feel-good moment. And chances are that as adults, we like it even less. But part of living a life of faith is being willing to makes changes in how we live and what we do. Once we accept Jesus as our Savior, God will use every opportunity to make us more like His Son. And while that's often a challenging path, it's also one laced with countless blessings.

The truth is, we get to choose. We can choose to be part of the sanctification process, or we can be part of the problem. We can open our heart to becoming more like Jesus, or we can be stubborn and set in our ways. But when we come to understand God is faithful and trustworthy, surrendering to His leading will be an easy choice. The Lord's discipline will be welcomed because it will prove we are His.

Father, I surrender to Your will in my life.
In Jesus' name I pray. Amen.

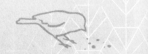

Lift Your Tired Hands

*So be made strong even in your weakness by lifting up
your tired hands in prayer and worship. And strengthen
your weak knees, for as you keep walking forward on God's
paths all your stumbling ways will be divinely healed!*

HEBREWS 12:12–13 TPT

There is something powerful about physically lifting our hands to the heavens, especially when we feel broken, battered, and bruised. It can be an act of surrender. For some it may be asking the Father to lift them into His arms, or a way to signal a need for comfort. For others it's a way to praise God for who He is, acknowledging their faith in His promise to bring comfort and healing. It may even be a prayer when words don't seem to come. And the most amazing part is that God knows exactly what it means.

Are you struggling in your marriage or as a mom? Are you scared by a doctor's report? Is your financial situation overwhelming? Is your career in shambles and you're out of options? Are your friendships changing and you're battling loneliness? Lift up your tired hands in prayer and watch as God's love responds.

**Father, I need Your comfort right now. I feel lost and have
no answers. I'm not sure how to move forward, and I'm
tired. Strengthen my faith to trust You as I wait for Your
help. I know it's coming. In Jesus' name I pray. Amen.**

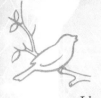

The Way to Contentment

*I know how to live on almost nothing or with everything. I have
learned the secret of contentment in every situation, whether it be a full
stomach or hunger, plenty or want; for I can do everything God asks
me to with the help of Christ who gives me the strength and power.*

PHILIPPIANS 4:12–13 TLB

When you keep faith at the front of your life, finding contentment will
be a whole lot easier. Why? Because your focus will be on eternal things
rather than worldly. You'll see the value in serving others over collecting
for yourself. You will understand the deeper, spiritual meaning behind
being rich and being poor. And you'll realize that God has promised to
meet every one of your needs in meaningful ways.

The truth is that your current circumstances should have no bearing
on the state of your faith. Let it thrive whether you are in a rough patch
or on cloud nine. It should be consistent regardless of your worries, fears,
or insecurities. It's a learning process, but if you trust the Lord, He will
teach you how to be a woman of faith no matter what is happening
around you. He'll show you ways to anchor your heart to Him so peace
reigns. You'll be able to find hope through the mess. And God will fill
you with power to stand strong, unwavering in your belief that you are
enough and that you have enough.

Father, teach me to be content based on You and not
my circumstances. I know You will give me every tool
I need to weather whatever storm comes my way. You
will bless me with what I need to find hope and joy and
peace even when life feels upside down. Amen.

When We Don't Want to Love

No matter what, make room in your heart to love every
believer. And show hospitality to strangers, for they may
be angels from God showing up as your guests.

HEBREWS 13:1–2 TPT

If God thought it important enough to include in His Word, then we need to take His command to love others seriously. Be it another believer or a complete stranger, God wants us to make room for them in our heart. Can we agree this is a tall order? Honestly, some people make themselves very hard to love. When we think about those who have hurt us or someone we care about, the idea of showing them kindness seems inauthentic. Being generous to strangers can feel awkward or forced. But when we activate our faith and ask God for the supernatural ability to love, He will give it.

Where are you struggling to extend grace, show kindness, or love fiercely? You don't need to have it all figured out. It's human to battle this concept. That's where faith comes into the picture. When we don't have the strength or desire, God will infuse us with it. Just ask.

Father, I want to live a righteous life, but I'm struggling to find the gumption to love the unlovable. I'm intimidated by the idea of being generous with strangers. Grow my faith so I can be courageous in the way I treat others. Let me be known as someone who loves well. In Jesus' name I pray. Amen.

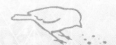

God Will Never Leave You

Stay away from the love of money; be satisfied with what you have.
For God has said, "I will never, never fail you nor forsake you." That
is why we can say without any doubt or fear, "The Lord is my Helper,
and I am not afraid of anything that mere man can do to me."

HEBREWS 13:5–6 TLB

How would you step out of your comfort zone if you knew God would never fail you? If you were assured of God's constant companionship, what would you try? Friend, He created you to be fearless. He made you bold in a special way. And it's your faith in His promises that will help you find the confidence to be who God made you to be.

Even more, nothing will separate you from Him. The Lord never leaves your side and says He will always help you. Let this promise grow your courage to experience new things. To speak up. To have the hard conversations. To try again. To forgive. To love yourself. It's time to be fearless, beloved, drawing your strength from God Himself. Let your faith rise up!

Father, help me anchor my confidence and courage in
You so I can live the life You've chosen for me. I want to
be a woman who is fearless and faithful. And I can't do
it without Your help! In Jesus' name I pray. Amen.

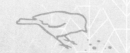

He Will Give You What You Need

Now may the God of peace who brought up our Lord Jesus from
the dead, that great Shepherd of the sheep, through the blood of
the everlasting covenant, make you complete in every good work
to do His will, working in you what is well pleasing in His sight,
through Jesus Christ, to whom be glory forever and ever. Amen.

HEBREWS 13:20–21 NKJV

If you need to forgive, God will give you the ability to extend grace. If He wants you to show love to someone, you'll receive divine compassion. If you need a measure of patience in a situation, God will fill you with endurance. If you need strength, wisdom, peace, or power, by faith you'll receive it. So in those moments when you feel like you don't have what it takes, go straight to God.

Don't waste time trying to muster these needs for yourself. You may dig a little up on your own, but it won't last for long. Instead, tell the Lord exactly what you are lacking and let Him bless you with it. You delight His heart when you're willing to humble yourself and ask for help to walk out the plan He has for your life.

Father, help me follow the plan You've made for my life.
I want to bring glory to Your holy name. I trust You'll give
me everything necessary to complete the work You've
established for me to do. In Jesus' name I pray. Amen.

The Confidence to Ask

If you don't have all the wisdom needed for this journey, then
all you have to do is ask God for it; and God will grant all that
you need. He gives lavishly and never scolds you for asking.

JAMES 1:5 VOICE

Sometimes we're embarrassed to ask the Lord for help. Maybe we've decided we should be able to handle it on our own. Maybe we've asked so many times we're sure He is exhausted by us. Or maybe we think our request is too small and trivial. But, friend, are these thoughts theologically sound? No.

God's Word is crystal clear. It tells us repeatedly that we should ask for what we need. He is a good Father who deeply loves His children. What good parent wouldn't want to equip their son or daughter to make them successful? Have faith in the Lord, choosing to believe His heart for you is always good. And have confidence to ask for wisdom, discernment, direction, endurance, and whatever else you need.

Father, thank You for inviting any and all of my requests.
In the past, I've been worried about asking too much
or too often. I've been insecure to open up. And so I've
looked to myself to figure it all out. But now I know I
am free to share my needs with You, trusting each one
will be met in love. In Jesus' name I pray. Amen.

An Increased Measure of Faith

"No matter how many times in one day your brother sins against
you and says, 'I'm sorry; I am changing; forgive me,' you need to
forgive him each and every time." Upon hearing this, the apostles
said to Jesus, "Lord, you must increase our measure of faith!"

LUKE 17:4–5 TPT

There are things in life we simply cannot do without faith. It's a prerequisite
to righteous living. Where our human abilities end, faith finishes. And
one of the most difficult things we're asked to do is forgive. We think it
lets our offender off the hook. We think it diminishes the pain we felt.
In truth, it releases us from the bondage that unforgiveness creates
because its power is taken away.

But just as the apostles needed to ask for an increase in faith to forgive,
we do too. Extending grace often takes more grit than we have because
the offense was deeply personal. The pain was almost unbearable, and
the last thing we want to do is forgive. But forgiveness is required and
expected, and when we ask for help, God will make it doable.

Father, there's nothing in me that wants to forgive
those who've hurt me. I confess that most of the time
I want to hurt them back. Please increase my faith so
I can draw on Your strength to forgive my offenders.
And change my heart so I deeply understand why
forgiveness is important. In Jesus' name I pray. Amen.

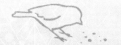

Asking in Faith

So [Jesus] asked [the boy's] father, "How long has this been happening to him?" And he said, "From childhood. And often he has thrown him both into the fire and into the water to destroy him. But if You can do anything, have compassion on us and help us." Jesus said to him, "If you can believe, all things are possible to him who believes."

MARK 9:21–23 NKJV

This father was desperate. His son was possessed by a demon and he'd watched helplessly as the condition persisted, feeling hopeless. If you're a parent, chances are you completely understand. Watching our kids struggle hurts deeply. But when this man found Jesus and begged for deliverance for his son, his lack of faith was revealed when he said to Jesus, "If you can do anything. . ."

How many times have you approached the Lord with the same attitude? Your request feels so big that you question if God can even handle it. It's a crisis of faith. Jesus was quick to respond and gently called the father out for his doubt. And in that moment Jesus reminded him (and us) that all things are possible when we ask in faith.

Father, I confess the times I've doubted Your ability. I'm sorry for thinking You are unable to be God. Help me know without question that You are sovereign and fully capable of anything. And remind me to lean into You when I'm feeling desperate for deliverance. I believe in Your power! In Jesus' name I pray. Amen.

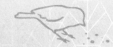

The Reward For Faith

I have fought an excellent fight. I have finished my full course with all my might and I've kept my heart full of faith. There's a crown of righteousness waiting in heaven for me, and I know that my Lord will reward me on his day of righteous judgment. And this crown is not only waiting for me, but for all who love and long for his unveiling.

2 TIMOTHY 4:7–8 TPT

There is a reward for having a heart full of faith. It's not a perfect life here on earth. It's not trouble-free relationships. It's not financial security or access to the fountain of youth. It's not the guarantee of winning or finding success at every turn. No, the reward you'll receive for faithful living will be given to you in heaven. It's a crown you'll wear for being right with God. And even more, He'll be the One to give it to you.

So while you're here, dig in your heels and choose to fight the good fight. Don't give up and walk away when things are hard. Don't let anyone or anything steal your solid faith in God, even though it may take all you have to hold on to it at times. Instead, choose to trust the Lord and know He will bless you richly for it.

Father, help me choose to activate my faith in You every time and in every situation. In Jesus' name I pray. Amen.

Faith Is Faith

*It's not like you need a huge amount of faith. If you just had
faith the size of a single, tiny mustard seed, you could say to this
huge tree, "Pull up your roots and replant yourself in the sea,"
and it would fly through the sky and do what you said. So even
a little faith can accomplish the seemingly impossible.*

LUKE 17:6 VOICE

Today's verse makes an important point. Sometimes we think our faith
must reach a certain place before we can take the next step. We wait or
opt out because we aren't as "Christian" as others. We feel immature in
our belief and give ourselves a free pass, deciding we have a ways to go
before we can trust at the level required.

Faith is faith. And be it small or large, it's backed by God's promises.
So even if our faith is new, it still has power. Even if we're just finding it
again, God honors it. And when we choose to believe these things to be
true, we can stand with confidence and activate it in any situation that
comes our way.

Father, I confess I've disqualified myself in the past
because I didn't feel like my faith was enough. I decided
it lacked the power to help me. I didn't believe it had the
maturity to pack a punch. But I know now that faith is
faith! And You will honor it! In Jesus' name I pray. Amen.

The Powerful Trio

But now faith, hope, and love remain; these three virtues
must characterize our lives. The greatest of these is love.

1 CORINTHIANS 13:13 VOICE

To be women of great faith, we're told to foster three specific qualities. And while the most important one is love, faith and hope are a close second and third. These work in concert together, and it's a beautiful combination that helps us make our life count. Do they come naturally? Most likely not. But they can be firmly established in you.

Let God build up this powerful trio in you. Let Him be the One to nurture and mature them into something to behold—something that becomes second nature. Now and then you may struggle to allow faith, hope, and love to characterize your life, but time with God will help. Intentional living will help too. And focusing on these virtues will bless not only you but also all those around you.

Father, help me grow in faith, hope, and love. Sometimes I see flashes of them in my life, but they don't always come easily. Please firmly plant them in me so they will eventually mature and bloom. I want this powerful trio to describe, distinguish, and define me. I want to be known for them because they point to Your goodness! And I know without Your time and attention, they will be impossible to cultivate. In Jesus' name I pray. Amen.

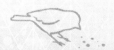

How to Be a Conqueror

Every God-born person conquers the world's ways. The conquering power that brings the world to its knees is our faith. The person who wins out over the world's ways is simply the one who believes Jesus is the Son of God.

1 JOHN 5:4–5 MSG

If you are a child of God—believing Jesus is the Son of God, died on the cross for your sins, and rose three days later—you have power. The world is no match because you have direct access to His strength. And your faith is what delivers the victory over anything that comes against you. It gives you conquering power for the battle.

Your victory doesn't come from your own plans. It doesn't come from gadgets or gizmos. You can't will it to be or cross your fingers and hope. It has nothing to do with how many people stand with you or the number of books you've read on the topic. The one who conquers the world is the one who chooses to believe Jesus really is the Son of God. Victory comes through faith.

> Father, I believe Jesus is Your Son. But so often I forget that belief makes me an overcomer. I forget the victory it affords me. Help me grab hold of the blessings that come from being Your child. Help me stand in faith and win out over the world's ways! In Jesus' name I pray. Amen.

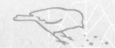

A State of Stillness

"Be still, be calm, see, and understand I am the True God. I am honored among all the nations. I am honored over all the earth."

PSALM 46:10 VOICE

It takes faith to be still when life around you feels chaotic. When your world is on a roller coaster ride, choosing to be calm seems almost impossible. When relationships, finances, and work are unsettled, stress can take a toll. But the Lord is right there, asking You to believe *He* is God, not you. It's not your job to figure it all out on your own. You're not in charge of fixing it. Instead, trusting God with everything makes the impossible possible.

Think about situations that feel overwhelming. What circumstances fill your heart with worry? Are you stressing over things out of your control? Friend, activate your faith and ask God to intervene. Take a step back, recognizing His divine position over your earthly one. And understand that God will help you find a state of stillness while He makes all things right.

> Father, it's not natural for me to be still when my life is falling apart. I'm a doer and a fixer, and I confess there are times I feel god-like because I take control. But I'm asking You to bring me to a state of stillness so I can honor Your power and strength in my life. I want You to be the One in control. In Jesus' name I pray. Amen.

Faith Heals

Jesus responded, "Your faith heals you. Go in peace, with your sight restored." All at once, the man's eyes opened and he could see again, and he began at once to follow Jesus, walking down the road with him.

MARK 10:52 TPT

Did you know your faith brings healing? Choosing to believe in God's strength and power sets you up for miracles. And today's passage of scripture reminds us we don't have to see Him working to trust that He is. The blind man didn't see the Lord at work. His faith allowed him to just. . .*believe.*

Where are you struggling to know God is moving in your situation? What have you been asking for that you haven't seen come to pass yet? Having faith means you know His hands are in your circumstances. You trust He's working all things out for your good. You believe God is gracious, kind, and attentive to the needs you've placed before Him. And with that faith comes confidence in His healing power, His perfect timing, and His hope-filled plans for your life.

Father, grow my faith so I can believe in Your miracles without any doubt. Help me trust You always have my best interests in mind. Open my heart to receive Your help and healing at the right time. And build my confidence, reminding me that my faith in You brings with it beautiful blessings and rewards because of Your goodness! In Jesus' name I pray. Amen.

A Powerful Combination for Living

Keep your eyes open, hold tight to your convictions,
give it all you've got, be resolute, and love without stopping.

1 CORINTHIANS 16:13–14 MSG

Today's verse is concise and packed with a powerful combination for living and loving well. We are told to be careful and keep our eyes open so we can clearly see what's ahead. We're to be strong in our faith and convictions so we don't waver in weakness. We are to be full of courage and try our hardest in every situation, and we are to be full of resolve so we don't give up. And all we do is to be done in love.

Is this a tall order? Yes! But, friend, that's why you trust God. He is the One who brings the *super* to your *natural*. Your faith is what opens you up to His strength and power. It unlocks endurance and wisdom. And it's because God first loved you that your heart can be tender toward others.

Father, thank You for a road map for how to live
a faithful, righteous life. I love that You don't mince
words and provide clear direction. Now help me walk
out this path with intentionality and to be a warrior
for the faith in all I do! In Jesus' name I pray. Amen.

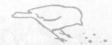

Let God Reign

*Now may God, the fountain of hope, fill you to overflowing with
uncontainable joy and perfect peace as you trust in him. And
may the power of the Holy Spirit continually surround your life
with his super-abundance until you radiate with hope!*

ROMANS 15:13 TPT

What a blessing to realize that when we place our trust in God, we have access to joy and peace. Honestly, letting go like that is a brave act of surrender. It's deciding we just don't have what it takes to do what needs to be done, but the Lord does. It's choosing to step aside and let God be God because we are not. It's taking the weight of worry off our shoulders and laying it at His feet, knowing He will work for our good. Best of all, this act of faith brings peace and joy with it.

God is fully capable of bringing healing, restoration, or closure to your circumstances. He can soften hearts, open or close doors, and provide a new perspective. Let your faith bring encouragement to let go and let God reign in your life.

Father, I'm trusting You with tough situations and asking
for an overflow of joy and peace. Reign in my life and fill my
heart with hope. I am letting go of the control and trusting
You for every need right now. In Jesus' name I pray. Amen.

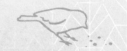

Being Right with God

But we know that no one is made right with God by meeting the demands
of the law. It is only through the faithfulness of Jesus the Anointed that
salvation is even possible. This is why we put faith in Jesus the Anointed: so
we will be put right with God. It's His faithfulness—not works prescribed
by the law—that puts us in right standing with God because no one will
be acquitted and declared "right" for doing what the law demands.

GALATIANS 2:16 VOICE

What a relief to realize we cannot become righteous based on our actions.
Being a slave to a set of rules (the law) is a setup for failure, because our
human condition makes it impossible to be perfect. How kind of God to
make another way, one that asks us to have faith instead. By choosing to
anchor our faith in Jesus as the Son of God over any performance-based
expectation, we are made right with the Father.

You don't have to be flawless. God isn't keeping score or hoping
your life is impeccable. Instead, He invites you to come to Him messy
and imperfect. Trust God with it all and believe that your faith in Him
is what makes you righteous.

Father, thank You for not expecting me to be perfect in my
actions. I would fail within the hour. I'm so grateful that instead,
Your Son made faith possible for me. In Jesus' name I pray. Amen.

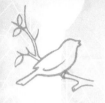

The Shield of Faith

*In every battle you will need faith as your shield
to stop the fiery arrows aimed at you by Satan.*

EPHESIANS 6:16 TLB

Your faith is a shield against the enemy's arrows. In your mind's eye, can you see a picture of you holding up that shield of protection as the devil is firing arrows of lies and destruction your way? Can you feel them hit the shield and immediately lose power as they fall to the ground? Rather than hitting you where it would hurt the most, those arrows are rendered useless as your faith in God ruins the enemy's plans.

When Satan wants to discourage you from stepping out of your comfort zone, God gives you courage. When he wants to ruin your friendship, God gives you grace. When the enemy wants you to doubt your abilities, God gives you confidence. As long as you stay behind your shield of faith—growing in your relationship with Him—the enemy loses power. He may wreak havoc in your life, but never in your heart.

Father, thank You for equipping me with a shield of faith
as protection from the enemy's arrows. Boy, does he try to
discourage me daily, but I know my faith in You leaves him
powerless every time. My strength to stand strong comes from
You. My hope lies in You. And my courage and confidence
are anchored in Your truths. In Jesus' name I pray. Amen.

The Destruction of Doubt

Just make sure you ask empowered by confident faith without doubting that you will receive. For the ambivalent person believes one minute and doubts the next. Being undecided makes you become like the rough seas driven and tossed by the wind. You're up one minute and tossed down the next.

JAMES 1:6 TPT

Doubt is very destructive because it works against your faith. It makes you uncertain of God's willingness and ability. You begin to question if He can do what He says He'll do. And rather than trust the Lord, you hesitate. But He wants your requests to be big and bold. He wants you to ask for what you need with confidence. God expects your prayers to be empowered by confident faith.

Scripture says that asking God for help but doubting a response is like being tossed around in rough seas. It will be terribly destabilizing. How will that help you at all? So, friend, when you pray, be brave and choose to believe God hears you and will respond. Push doubt aside and activate your faith instead.

> Father, I confess the times I've come to You with doubt in my heart. Forgive me for not remembering Your awesomeness. From today forward, I'm going to stand strong in my faith and know that You are God. Not only do You hear me, but You will always provide the right response at the right time. In Jesus' name I pray. Amen.

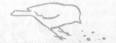

41

Living by Faith

"Behold the proud, His soul is not upright in him;
but the just shall live by his faith."

HABAKKUK 2:4 NKJV

If we boast in our own abilities, trusting ourselves over God, we will eventually meet with failure. But it should be the other way around. Having faith means we choose to trust Him instead. It's not that we're worthless or unable. We're just not God. And our trust should be solidly anchored in the only One who can meet us where we are and help us cross the finish line.

Let God guide you to parent your challenging child. Let Him give you creative ideas in your job. Let the Lord fill you with motivation to better your health. And ask Him for grace and energy in relationships. Relying on God for these kinds of things defines you as a faithful woman. It testifies of your belief in His power because you are walking out your faith in real time. So choose today whom you will trust for the small things and big things. It matters.

Father, help me choose to trust You rather than
always relying on myself. It's exhausting trying to figure
everything out, and I don't always do a good job of it. I want
to be the kind of woman who is faithful and understands
the limits I'm bound by. In Jesus' name I pray. Amen.

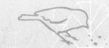

The True Colors of Your Faith

*Consider it a sheer gift, friends, when tests and challenges
come at you from all sides. You know that under pressure, your
faith-life is forced into the open and shows its true colors. So don't
try to get out of anything prematurely. Let it do its work so you
become mature and well-developed, not deficient in any way.*

JAMES 1:2–4 MSG

When you find yourself burdened by stress and strife, there is no doubt
your faith will show its true colors. Anxiety will reveal the exact strength
of it. Worry will expose the actual maturity of it. Insecurities will uncover
the real depth of it. And fear will disclose the true reliability of it. Yep.
Tests and challenges will force your faith into the open.

Spend time now growing your relationship with God. Open your
Bible to see what it says. Talk to Him in prayer, sharing every heartbreak
and struggle. Take your needs to Him and watch as God provides for
each one. These build faith into something sustainable that will hold
you up when life gets tough. And just like most everything else, the time
you sow will reap beautiful benefits.

Father, when the hard seasons hit, I want my
revealed faith to be authentic. I want it to point
to You in heaven. I want it to encourage those
around me. Let it be! In Jesus' name I pray. Amen.

The Lord Satisfies

I am the bread that gives life. If you come to My table and eat,
you will never go hungry. Believe in Me, and you will never go thirsty.

JOHN 6:35 VOICE

Your faith in the Lord will be what satisfies you. Friend, do you truly believe this? The world offers a buffet of options that promise to meet our needs. Countless earthly opportunities are selling hope and trying to catch our attention. But Jesus boldly proclaimed that He is the One who will quench us at the foundational level.

So where do you go to find contentment? Who are the friends or family you rely on to fill you up? What meets your needs on a regular basis? While we may look to community, working out, volunteering, church, food, or something else to help, Jesus is what sustains us without fail. Let your faith rise up when your spirit is hungry or thirsty. The Lord is always ready to bless you!

Father, forgive me for looking to the world's offerings to fill the needs only You can meet. I'm guilty of picking other things over You, and I want to change that. Give me confidence to always look to You as my sustainer and provider. And help me remember my faith in You comes with blessings. I believe in You and I trust You. You are all I need. In Jesus' name I pray. Amen.

Focus on Jesus

*We look away from the natural realm and we focus our attention
and expectation onto Jesus who birthed faith within us and who
leads us forward into faith's perfection. His example is this: Because
his heart was focused on the joy of knowing that you would be his,
he endured the agony of the cross and conquered its humiliation,
and now sits exalted at the right hand of the throne of God!*

HEBREWS 12:2 TPT

Keeping our attention focused on the Lord is critical because He is our true north. He keeps our heart healthy when our expectations are anchored in Him. And when life feels out of control, our eyes should be looking to Him for hope. Too often we lean into the things of the world to help us feel better, but they can't deliver the life-changing remedies that bring peace.

Let Jesus be the perfecter of your faith. He has skin in the game—literally. He went to the cross knowing His sacrifice had to happen to make you one of His. He was tortured. Beaten. Bloodied. But Jesus' heart was focused on you. That's why your heart can now be focused on Him.

**Father, I'm humbled just thinking of all You did to ensure
a relationship with me. Your Son died so I'd be able to
anchor my faith in You. Keep this truth top of mind for me.
I never want to forget it. In Jesus' name I pray. Amen.**

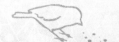

Run Hard and Fast

But you, Timothy, man of God: Run for your life from all this. Pursue
a righteous life—a life of wonder, faith, love, steadiness, courtesy. Run
hard and fast in the faith. Seize the eternal life, the life you were called to,
the life you so fervently embraced in the presence of so many witnesses.

1 TIMOTHY 6:11–12 MSG

Be the kind of woman who runs hard and fast in the faith. Live with bold belief in who God is, knowing He will do what He says He'll do. Pursue a life that's right with God where you're purposeful to walk out your faith every day and in all situations. Live unhindered by the worries of the world as you cling to the Lord for deliverance, and love others with passion as you see them through His eyes of care and kindness.

Take advantage of every opportunity to surrender control into God's hands, and watch with expectation as He straightens the crooked path of life. And remember others are watching you, so live your faith in God out loud as a powerful testimony of His goodness.

Father, give me endurance to run hard and fast as I live
out my faith. Let my life encourage others to pursue You
with all they have. Help me focus on keeping You at the
center so I can walk out the purpose You have placed
on my life. I'm all in. In Jesus' name I pray. Amen.

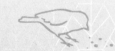

Great Is Your Faith

*Then Jesus answered and said to her, "O woman,
great is your faith! Let it be to you as you desire."
And her daughter was healed from that very hour.*

MATTHEW 15:28 NKJV

Jesus rewarded this mom's faith by completely healing her daughter. He saw in her a desperation for restoration. He saw a relentless belief in what He could do. Jesus recognized her deep confidence in Him, and He honored it. And in the end, her daughter was made whole again because she chose to cling to her faith over everything else.

Where are you anxious for God's intervention in your own life? Do you need His help in piecing back together a broken relationship? Stabilizing your finances? Finding relief from a health issue? Maybe you need help moving past grief or unforgiveness. Are you stuck in a cycle of sin? Follow this woman's example and take your need straight to God, letting Him see your great faith in knowing He can and will meet your need.

Father, grow my faith to be as strong as the faith of the
mom in today's verse. I love that her belief was relentless!
Teach me to set my mind on Your power to heal and restore,
and help me cling to it with all I've got. I don't want good
faith—I want great faith! In Jesus' name I pray. Amen.

It's Not Up to You!

Seeing his reaction, Jesus said, "Do you have any idea how difficult it is for people who have it all to enter God's kingdom? I'd say it's easier to thread a camel through a needle's eye than get a rich person into God's kingdom." "Then who has any chance at all?" the others asked. "No chance at all," Jesus said, "if you think you can pull it off by yourself. Every chance in the world if you trust God to do it."

LUKE 18:24–27 MSG

A common misconception among people is that we get to heaven through our own efforts. We think we must be perfect with the words we speak. We decide our actions must be fueled by the right motives. And we believe our performance here on earth is what makes or breaks our entrance into eternity with God. But the Word is clear that we don't enter His kingdom by being good enough. It's not up to us. . .praise the Lord!

The truth is that the only way you will enter heaven is through faith alone—through choosing to place your trust in Jesus as your Savior. And your faith is enough!

> Father, what a huge relief to know my salvation
> is not up to me. Thank You that eternity doesn't
> depend on anything I do. I believe in You and trust
> You as my Savior. In Jesus' name I pray. Amen.

Mighty Faith

He never stopped believing God's promise, for he was made
strong in his faith to father a child. And because he was
mighty in faith and convinced that God had all the power
needed to fulfill his promises, Abraham glorified God!

ROMANS 4:20–21 TPT

Abraham never had doubt in his God. He knew deep down on a cellular level that the Lord would keep every promise made, and so this amazing man of God believed without fail. His faith was mighty! Abraham trusted that his God had the power necessary to do what He said He would do. And this resolve allowed him to give praise and glory to the Lord without a hint of hesitation.

Do you hesitate in your belief? Are there times in prayer when you wonder if God is listening or if He will respond? Have you asked Him for help but felt certain it wasn't going to come? Have you given up on a promise from God because it has taken too long? Choose today to ask God to grow your faith to be mighty! If you're going to err, err on the side of believing God.

Father, remove doubt in me of Your goodness and faithfulness. Give me the courage to trust that You will do what You say You'll do. Do whatever it takes to convince me that with You, promises made are promises kept. In Jesus' name I pray. Amen.

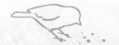

Live by Believing

"Martha," Jesus said, "you don't have to wait until then. I am the
Resurrection, and I am Life Eternal. Anyone who clings to me
in faith, even though he dies, will live forever. And the one who
lives by believing in me will never die. Do you believe this?"

JOHN 11:25–26 TPT

Choose to be someone who lives by believing. When the bad news comes, believe that God is already in the circumstances working things out. When the betrayal is discovered, trust that He is aware of your broken heart and will put it back together. When your life feels overwhelming and hopeless, let faith push you toward the peace of Jesus. When important relationships begin failing, cry out for God's intervention as you work toward reconciliation.

Not only is belief in God's goodness the right posture and mindset for facing your day-to-day struggles, but it's also the product of a faith anchored by a saving relationship with Jesus. When you choose to live by believing in the Lord, you can look forward with confidence to a beautiful eternity in heaven.

Father, thank You for Jesus and the gift of salvation that
comes from believing in Him. Help me walk out that belief
every day. Teach me to lean on You as I trust that Your
hand is at work in my life. And grow my faith so it's what
I'll cling to in tough times. In Jesus' name I pray. Amen.

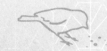

Fearless Faith

Even in the unending shadows of death's darkness, I am not
overcome by fear. Because You are with me in those dark moments,
near with Your protection and guidance, I am comforted.

PSALM 23:4 VOICE

You need bold faith to walk out today's verse. Showing nothing but courage when the deepest darkness overtakes your life requires a tremendous amount of grit. For many of us, fear is where we land when we get the phone call or walk away from a hard conversation. It's the emotion that floods in after we get laid off or file for bankruptcy. Fear is familiar to every one of us.

How can we have the kind of faith that overcomes fearful reactions? The reality is it comes from time spent with the Lord. It comes from soaking in His promises, like the ones saying you're never without His presence. It's taking a moment to pause and pray for His comfort, His protection, and His guidance. It's believing that His presence with you makes a difference. And it's asking Him to grow in you a bold faith.

Father, sometimes fear gains a foothold in my life and
pulls me in the opposite direction of faith. The two
cannot coexist. Please give me confidence that You are
alive and active in my life. You're intimately involved in
the details of my scary situations. Let me anchor myself
to that powerful truth. In Jesus' name I pray. Amen.

God Is Your Protector

You spread out a table before me, provisions in the midst of attack from my enemies; You care for all my needs, anointing my head with soothing, fragrant oil, filling my cup again and again with Your grace. Certainly Your faithful protection and loving provision will pursue me where I go, always, everywhere. I will always be with the Eternal, in Your house forever.

PSALM 23:5–6 VOICE

God is your protector. He's the One who will scoop you up from the chaos and carry you through it. His ears are trained on your voice, and He will respond every time you cry out to Him. God isn't bothered by your enemies because He is above all. Those who oppose you don't intimidate the Lord. As a matter of fact, scripture says He will give you exactly what you need to endure and overcome.

Don't cower under the pressure. Don't allow anyone to back you into a corner. You're the daughter of the King—the One who promises faithful protection and loving provision. So be intentional to grow in your faith and connect more deeply with God. Trust and believe in Him forever.

Father, thank You for caring for all my needs,
especially when the enemy is taunting me.
Sometimes I feel so unworthy of Your kindness
because I know I'm wretched without You.
Help me be confident as I ask for and accept Your
help in the hard seasons. In Jesus' name I pray. Amen.

Be Ready to Tell Them

Usually no one will hurt you for wanting to do good. But even if they should, you are to be envied, for God will reward you for it. Quietly trust yourself to Christ your Lord, and if anybody asks why you believe as you do, be ready to tell him, and do it in a gentle and respectful way.

1 PETER 3:13–15 TLB

When you're walking out your faith, others will notice. As followers of Jesus, we often respond to the world differently than those who don't follow Him. We have a peace that makes no sense to others. We can stand strong when tragedy hits home. We don't need comfort from others because we are held by the Lord Himself. Our perspective on hope and healing is different. And we're able to find moments of joy when it seems impossible to most.

Friend, be ready to answer for the difference in your life. When others notice something special about the way you live and love, trust that God will give you the words to share your faith. Simply tell them your story and how God intersected with it. Open up about the ways He has healed, restored, rescued, and changed you. Sharing your faith is a privilege!

Father, I will relish any opportunity to tell others about the ways You've blessed my life. I may be nervous, but my responsibility is to trust You for words and have a willing heart. I can do that. In Jesus' name I pray. Amen.

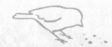

Faith in the Temptations

But remember this—the wrong desires that come into your
life aren't anything new and different. Many others have
faced exactly the same problems before you. And no temptation
is irresistible. You can trust God to keep the temptation from
becoming so strong that you can't stand up against it, for he has
promised this and will do what he says. He will show you how to
escape temptation's power so that you can bear up patiently against it.

1 CORINTHIANS 10:13 TLB

Have faith that God understands the struggles and temptations you face. In these, you aren't any different than anyone else. They are age-old battles many have faced before and will face after you. Every one of us grapples with challenges that feel so overwhelming they threaten to pull us under. And we will until we see Jesus face-to-face. It's just a fact.

But God won't leave you stuck in your struggles. He will make sure you are equipped to find freedom from every temptation. You may feel like you're going to buckle, but trust the Lord and cry out to Him. A promise from God is one that will be kept.

Father, I'm choosing to trust that You will deliver me from
the temptations that feel too heavy. Sometimes I feel like
I'm going to buckle beneath them. But You promise to
help, and I believe You! In Jesus' name I pray. Amen.

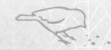

Embraced in the Faith

Welcome with open arms fellow believers who don't see things the
way you do. And don't jump all over them every time they do or say
something you don't agree with—even when it seems that they are
strong on opinions but weak in the faith department. Remember,
they have their own history to deal with. Treat them gently.

ROMANS 14:1 MSG

Be careful not to be prideful in your faith. Don't look down on those who aren't as seasoned as you. Remember, you were there once too. You've gradually grown in the faith and deepened your understanding of the Lord. As with anything else, following God is a learned process. So don't discount the ideas or insights of a young Christian, assuming they don't know as much as you. Instead, reach your hand back and help them along.

What an encouragement you can be to your fellow believers when you don't judge them as newbies. How wonderful for them to be able to ask questions and feel embraced in the faith. Welcome those with differing opinions with open arms and no judgment. We all want to belong and feel part of something bigger than ourselves, so be the kind of woman who welcomes authentic faith no matter what.

Father, help me be someone who greets others in the faith
with open arms. Give me a heart for them so I can embrace
them right where they are. In Jesus' name I pray. Amen.

God Is Your Source

*And I pray that he would unveil within you the unlimited riches of his
glory and favor until supernatural strength floods your innermost being
with his divine might and explosive power. Then, by constantly using
your faith, the life of Christ will be released deep inside you, and the
resting place of his love will become the very source and root of your life.*

<small>EPHESIANS 3:16–17 TPT</small>

God's hope is that you will constantly use your faith. What does that
mean? It means that you see God as your source for everything. Whatever
comes your way, you go to the Lord with it. You let Him be the solution.
You train yourself to trust God to be what you need. It's having confidence He will come through at the right time and in the right way.
And when you walk this out, the very source and root of your life will
be the Lord.

God has unlimited riches in store for those who consistently flex
their faith muscles. Through His Spirit, you will be strengthened. His
love will define your life and become its foundation. And God will bless
you as you make Him the resounding source of your bold and confident faith.

> Father, You are my source. Nothing the world offers
> comes anywhere close to You. Teach me to use my
> faith constantly and allow Your love to become the
> foundation of my life. In Jesus' name I pray. Amen.

Faith like Sarah's

*By faith Abraham's wife Sarah became fertile long after menopause because
she believed God would be faithful to His promise. So from this man,
who was almost at death's door, God brought forth descendants, as many
as the stars in the sky and as impossible to count as the sands of the shore.*

HEBREWS 11:11–12 VOICE

Talk about believing for a miracle. Menopause was over and Sarah still chose to believe that God could perform the impossible—at least by human standards—and make her a mother. Friend, that is a beautiful example of faith. And it's also a huge challenge for any mere mortal to walk out. But if Sarah and Abraham could believe with such certainty, so can we.

Where are you looking for a miracle right now? What feels so overwhelming that holding on to hope for restoration feels silly? Stop right now and talk to God. Open your heart to Him and unpack your fears and frustrations. Let Him see your hopelessness. Show Him your despair. And ask God to give you faith like Sarah's to stand and believe in His sovereignty.

Father, I confess my lack of faith that things can change. Honestly, I am struggling to believe miracles even exist. Grow my belief in Your complete authority so I can live expecting Your hand to move in my life in meaningful ways. I want to have unwavering faith in Your goodness. In Jesus' name I pray. Amen.

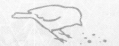

The Blessing of Suffering

*Suffering tests your faith which is more valuable than gold
(remember that gold, although it is perishable, is tested by fire) so
that if it is found genuine, you can receive praise, honor, and glory
when Jesus the Anointed, our Liberating King, is revealed at last.*

1 PETER 1:7 VOICE

We will all go through difficult seasons. This life is chock-full of ups
and downs, ebbs and flows, that often leave us freaking out. We face
overwhelming fear about horrible outcomes. We decide things won't
end well, so we give up and walk away. Some may seclude themselves
and suffer alone. And others may play the victim card to garner as much
attention as possible. People respond to suffering in many ways, but there
is only one answer to it: God.

The Lord allows suffering because even though it hurts, it brings
beautiful benefits. He uses it to deepen your faith as you cling to Him
for survival. In times of suffering, God becomes your soft landing. He's
your go-to. He is the One you ask for help because you realize He
really is all you've got. That kind of faith delights the Lord, and He will
bless you for it.

**Father, I don't like suffering but it's always where I
feel closest to You. Thank You for meeting me in it and
blessing me because of it. In Jesus' name I pray. Amen.**

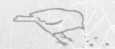

God or Money?

*"You can't worship two gods at once. Loving one god, you'll
end up hating the other. Adoration of one feeds contempt
for the other. You can't worship God and Money both."*

MATTHEW 6:24 MSG

When we spend time stressing and worrying about our financial situation—be it our current situation or in the future—it becomes an object of worship. Because our focus is fixed on our lack, it becomes an idol of sorts. As we give it our full attention, it drives us to obsess about ways we can make more or spend less. We read about it. Talk about it. Think about it. And somehow in the mix, we end up removing our need for God and placing the burden on our own shoulders instead.

But today's verse speaks clearly when it says we can't worship God and money at the same time. Either we're going to trust that God will provide, or we'll toil endlessly. Either we'll pray and wait for direction, or we'll try to fix our finances ourselves. Either our focus will be on God's sovereignty, or it won't. Ask Him to grow your faith muscles so you can flex your belief and worship Him alone.

Father, I'm surrendering to Your authority over my finances.
Direct me so I'm working with You rather than taking on
fear and stress alone. I trust You'll provide everything I
need. Help me cling to the assurance of Your provision
when fear rises up. In Jesus' name I pray. Amen.

The Perfect Timing of God

This is GOD's Word on the subject: "As soon as Babylon's seventy years are up and not a day before, I'll show up and take care of you as I promised and bring you back home. I know what I'm doing. I have it all planned out—plans to take care of you, not abandon you, plans to give you the future you hope for."

JEREMIAH 29:10–11 MSG

God's timing is perfect. While sometimes it may feel like it, He is never late to a situation and He doesn't intervene too soon. He always steps in at the exact right time. Because God can see the whole situation with full understanding, be confident He'll show up and take care of things without fail. God plans to give you the future you hope for, which means you can trust He is fully invested in your life.

Are you at the eleventh hour, friend? Are you at the end of your rope and barely hanging on? This is where your faith has the opportunity to shine. You may not know how things will turn out, but you know God is with you. You can trust He is working things out. And you can have peace knowing your life is of the utmost importance to Him. Share your heart with God and ask for peace in the waiting.

Father, I fully trust You and Your perfect
timing. In Jesus' name I pray. Amen.

It's a Privilege!

He entered into the world he created, yet the world was unaware. He came to the people he created—to those who should have received him, but they did not recognize him. But those who embraced him and took hold of his name he gave authority to become the children of God!

John 1:10–12 TPT

What a privilege to know the Lord. How wonderful to have eyes to see His fingerprints all over your life and ears to hear His still, small voice, because so many don't. They choose not to. And while Jesus came into the world with the sole intention of saving humankind, many people in those days showed no interest. They just didn't believe or care. Imagine how that kind of rejection must have felt then, and recognize the truth that it's still happening today.

But, friend, you embraced the Lord. Because you chose to believe in Jesus and accept Him as your personal Savior, He now calls you a child of God. Your identity is settled. Your faith has made you righteous, not perfect. And every time you cry out for His help or ask for His guidance, your request is heard in the heavens. Never be ashamed of following Him. It's a privilege!

Father, thank You for sending Your Son into the world to save me. I am so grateful to know You and worship You with my life. What an honor to be called a child of God. In Jesus' name I pray. Amen.

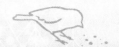

He Gets the Credit

*Give Him the credit for everything you accomplish, and He
will smooth out and straighten the road that lies ahead.*

PROVERBS 3:6 VOICE

Be careful you don't boast in your successes. Steer away from being a
braggart, taking credit for the skills and talents you possess. No one likes
individuals who toot their own horn or pat themselves on the back for
a job well done. Self-praise is unattractive and unfounded, and we should
be intentional to avoid acting this way at all costs. Life shouldn't be all
about us. It's about God.

So let's be quick to recognize that while we may be capable, smart,
and creative, God is the One who has blessed us. He has equipped us to
be remarkable. And while we put in the work and strive for excellence,
it's important we recognize all good things come from above, and that's
why we praise Him for what we're able to accomplish. It's why we ask
His help to straighten the road ahead. And it's why we rely on God's
guidance throughout our life.

Father, I confess the times I have taken full credit for the
good works in my life. I've used these moments to satisfy
insecurities, and I apologize. Help me give You the glory for
what I am able to accomplish. Thank You for creating me
with notable abilities. Please show me where and how to
use them to bring You glory. In Jesus' name I pray. Amen.

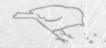

Believing and Speaking

For it is by believing in his heart that a man becomes
right with God; and with his mouth he tells others
of his faith, confirming his salvation.

ROMANS 10:10 TLB

Having faith in the Lord means you choose to believe in who He is with your heart. When He proclaims Himself the Creator of heaven and earth, you agree. When God says Jesus is His Son whose death paid the price for your sins, you accept His words as truth. When the Lord promises to protect, restore, heal, and sustain you, you trust Him. And when He offers you access to His wisdom, peace, and joy, you are confident in them. These choices make you right with God.

When you have certainty in who God is and what He can do, your mouth will speak it. Your words will reflect the faith you have that the Lord will come through once again. You'll discover countless opportunities to tell others about the way God has moved in your life. And the power of your testimony will reveal the saving relationship you have with Him.

Father, I do believe in who You are, and I trust in what
You say. Give me the confidence and the opportunities
to share my faith with those around me. Let me be a light
that shines brightly for You. In Jesus' name I pray. Amen.

Longing for Heaven

Now we look forward with confidence to our heavenly bodies,
realizing that every moment we spend in these earthly bodies is
time spent away from our eternal home in heaven with Jesus.
We know these things are true by believing, not by seeing.

2 CORINTHIANS 5:6–7 TLB

There's no doubt you are here for a reason. When God looked at His kingdom calendar, He decided this present time was when you'd be on Planet Earth. And knowing that, He equipped you for this day and age. God made you on purpose and for a purpose. Everything about you is by design. You were made to shine Jesus into the world, and that doesn't keep you from loving life and enjoying what it brings. But as women of faith, we also should have a deep longing to be at home in heaven with our Father. We should long for eternity while we walk out our faith here. We can do both—look forward and live faithfully—at the same time.

Every day we're here is time spent away from our heavenly home, but we honor God by choosing to walk the path He has paved. Faith reminds us to follow the Lord's leading and trust His timing. And we can be faithful in our life here while also longing for the eternal life we'll experience in heaven.

Father, I can hardly wait to be with You in heaven forever,
but I will trust Your timing! In Jesus' name I pray. Amen.

New Life through Faith

Then Jesus said to the woman, "Your faith in me has given
you life. Now you may leave and walk in the ways of peace."

LUKE 7:50 TPT

Choosing to place your faith in the Lord changes you. It might be subtle at first, but over time you'll notice some amazing differences in the way you handle the challenges that come your way. Where there used to be stress and worry, now you find peace. Where once there was anger, now you find grace. Instead of fear, you find the courage to stand tall. Rather than insecurity, you radiate with confidence. Something beautiful happens when you choose God. A new lease on life emerges—one that gives you purpose and passion.

Think back to your life before you received Jesus as your Savior. Remember how you handled difficult relationships. How you responded to tough circumstances. How you navigated grueling seasons when you felt hopeless. With your faith now anchored in Jesus, chances are you feel peace. You trust God is moving. You know He recognizes your pain. See, friend, your faith has given you a new life.

Father, I'm so grateful that my faith in You has brought about a noticeable change in me. It's more proof that You are alive and active, making me more like Christ every day. Let my life glorify You in the way I live it. In Jesus' name I pray. Amen.

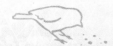

God Will Take Care of Everything

You can be sure that God will take care of everything you need, his
generosity exceeding even yours in the glory that pours from Jesus. Our
God and Father abounds in glory that just pours out into eternity. Yes.

PHILIPPIANS 4:19–20 MSG

It's okay, friend. You may be scared about what you think is coming next.
You may be worried things won't work out the way you want them to.
You may be anxious about the way everything will come together in the
end. Maybe you're looking at your needs, scared to death they won't be
met. Truth is, life is hard and unpredictable. But never forget that God
has made you a promise that is irrevocable: He will most certainly take
care of you without fail.

When you're struggling to believe everything will be okay, let your
faith rise up. Cry out to the Lord and tell Him every fear and insecurity
tormenting you. Share your worries and anxious thoughts with God.
And let Him be the One to reinforce your ability to trust that He will
take care of all things.

Father, help me find confidence through my faith
to know You will meet every need I have. Help me
trust that You're fully aware of the places I am lacking.
Reveal Your unmatched power in my life, and let it be an
encouragement to all who witness it. In Jesus' name I pray. Amen.

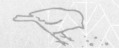

The Power of His Presence

This is My command: be strong and courageous. Never be afraid or discouraged because I am your God, the Eternal One, and I will remain with you wherever you go.

JOSHUA 1:9 VOICE

God's command here is absolute. He's telling us to be strong and courageous, no matter what. There are no exceptions. There's no opt-out button. There is no wiggle room. We don't get a free pass based on the circumstances we're facing. The Lord is calling us higher. He is calling us to rise up in faith and trust, because He will be a constant companion as we journey through life.

Don't underestimate the power of His presence. Do you realize that the God who created the heavens and the earth and everything in them chooses to stay with you? No matter where life takes you, and regardless of the battles that come, He will never leave. Through the tears, God is there. When your heart is broken, He is there. During seasons of doubt, the Lord is with you. And, friend, that is how you are able to stand with courage and hope.

Father, fear and discouragement have been part of my life forever, and I can hardly imagine being free of them altogether. But I do take Your commands seriously, which is why I'm asking for an awareness of Your presence. Let me feel Your courage and confidence coursing through my veins. Help me be brave. In Jesus' name I pray. Amen.

Don't Shrink Back

And those whose faith has made them good in God's sight
must live by faith, trusting him in everything. Otherwise,
if they shrink back, God will have no pleasure in them.

HEBREWS 10:38 TLB

If you want to please the Lord, trust Him in every area of your life. Let Him be the One you go to for help and healing in your relationships, finances, marriage, parenting, and health. Let Him be the One who knows every fear that overwhelms you. Tell God the ways life is shaking you up, and wait for His intervention with reverent expectation. Let the Lord see your bold faith revealed. When has He ever let you down? The reality is He never has and never will.

But understand that what will cause God displeasure is watching you shrink back when the storms rage. Because of your faith, you're not a wimp. You're not without hope. So the moment your faith begins to shrivel up, reengage with God. Be honest and ask for a greater level of trust. As a woman who believes, you don't have room for doubt to take root. . .so don't let it.

Father, grow me into a powerful woman of faith. Help me trust
that You are working in my life. I want to lean into Your ways
more every day. Show me how to stand strong so life doesn't
make me shrink back in cowardice. I trust You and I believe in
You. Seal that resolve in me today. In Jesus' name I pray. Amen.

Asking for More Faith

The father instantly replied, "I do have faith; oh, help me to
have more!" When Jesus saw the crowd was growing, he rebuked
the demon. "O demon of deafness and dumbness," he said, "I
command you to come out of this child and enter him no more!"

MARK 9:24–25 TLB

Don't be shy in asking God for more faith. There's nothing wrong with admitting that while you believe in God's power and strength, you need an extra measure of faith for this difficult season. You need a greater level of peace to deal with the challenges you're facing. You want to get anxiety under control. You're looking for confirmation God is working so you can find the courage to let go. You long to be comforted through the mess. Rest assured, asking the Lord to deepen your faith is an honest request He will reward.

Sometimes you will have full confidence as God is working in your situation. Belief will be a no-brainer, and a sense of calm will wash over you. But other times the stakes feel too high. The thought of relinquishing control feels too risky. The idea of surrendering seems too dangerous. It's in these times that asking for more faith reveals your maturity.

Father, I have faith. But in this situation, please help
me to have more! In Jesus' name I pray. Amen.

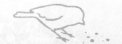

Faith That Works through Love

*But we have the true hope that comes from being made right
with God, and by the Spirit we wait eagerly for this hope. When
you're joined to the Anointed One, circumcision and religious
obligations can benefit you nothing. All that matters now is living
in the faith that works and expresses itself through love.*

GALATIANS 5:5–6 TPT

Part of walking out our faith is living a life that makes us right with
God. We know His plan is for us to become more like His Son, Jesus
Christ, and we wait eagerly for the Holy Spirit to mold us and shape
us through the process. It's not always a pleasant one, but it holds great
purpose and benefits us greatly in the end.

God wants us to have the kind of faith that works powerfully
through love. Loving others, after all, is the great command. Imagine
how different the world would be if love was our focus. It's putting others
first. It's being the hands and feet of God. It's meeting the needs of
those around us. It's speaking truth with the right intentions and motives.
And without faith and righteous living, it's impossible.

Father, make me more like Jesus so I can have the kind of
faith that expresses itself through love. Give me a heart
for others so my words and actions will help them be open
to hearing about You. In Jesus' name I pray. Amen.

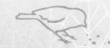

Let Him Carry Them

So bow down under God's strong hand; then when the
time comes, God will lift you up. Since God cares for you,
let Him carry all your burdens and worries.

1 Peter 5:6–7 voice

Have the kind of faith that trusts God with your worries. He not only wants to lighten your load but actually asks for it. Because God cares, He offers to remove the weight of worry from your shoulders and place it on His. But let's be honest: this act of surrender takes humility because it's often hard to admit we can't handle things on our own. We don't like to appear weak. We don't want others to think we're wimpy. And while we may not even realize it, our pridefulness keeps us from asking for help. Instead, we choose to carry our burdens alone.

Scripture says when we surrender to God, at the right time He will restore us. We will be lifted up because we chose to humble ourselves before Him. We recognized our position in relation to the Creator. And our faith is what will give us the courage to be vulnerable and transparent with God, sharing the worries troubling us.

Father, I confess my pride makes it hard to admit my worries
at times, and even harder to let another share my burdens.
Help my faith rise up so I will be quick to cry out for Your
help in those hard seasons. In Jesus' name I pray. Amen.

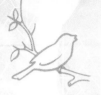

Take Faith Seriously

Our faith in Jesus transfers God's righteousness to us and he now declares us flawless in his eyes. This means we can now enjoy true and lasting peace with God, all because of what our Lord Jesus, the Anointed One, has done for us.

ROMANS 5:1 TPT

When you receive Jesus as your personal Savior, a powerful transformation takes place. His death on the cross paid the penalty for your sin, replacing it with a robe of righteousness. Jesus' blood washed you clean from every transgression—past, present, future—and allowed God to declare you flawless in His eyes. Jesus' selfless sacrifice makes it possible for you to have a relationship with the Lord.

In response, take your faith seriously. Be resolved to deepen your connection to God. Every day, make time to read and digest the Word, prioritize prayer, and worship your Father. Have a heart of gratitude toward Jesus' sacrifice, thanking Him daily. Share your heart with the Lord, inviting Him into your good and bad circumstances. Ask for renewed passion and purpose and be intentional to walk them out. And live and love in a way that reveals your thanks and praise to God. Let your faith rise up!

Father, help me be serious about deepening my relationship with You. Keep me focused on Your goodness so I have an attitude of gratitude. And thank You for all Jesus did for me. In His name I pray. Amen.

The Low-Lying Black Clouds

With the arrival of Jesus, the Messiah, that fateful dilemma is resolved. Those who enter into Christ's being-here-for-us no longer have to live under a continuous, low-lying black cloud. A new power is in operation. The Spirit of life in Christ, like a strong wind, has magnificently cleared the air, freeing you from a fated lifetime of brutal tyranny at the hands of sin and death.

ROMANS 8:1–2 MSG

What are the low-lying black clouds suffocating your life right now? Are you battling an addiction, unable to break free? Is anger becoming an issue, always boiling right under the surface? Are you in the midst of an active betrayal and can't find the courage to come clean? Let Jesus be the One to blow these clouds away.

Consider your faith like an air filter. Where you once lived surrounded by black clouds of fear, discouragement, and anxiety, believing in Jesus as your Savior brought a wind of change. You no longer have to live in the pollution of sin. Now you can breathe deeply and freely. What a difference faith makes!

Father, there are low-lying black clouds of sin in my life right now, and they're choking my joy. I'm not sure how I got here, but I'm stuck and need help. Let my belief in Jesus give me courage to deal with these issues so I can walk in freedom, breathing in the fresh air of faith. In Jesus' name I pray. Amen.

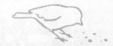

Permanent Access

*Our faith guarantees us permanent access into this
marvelous kindness that has given us a perfect relationship
with God. What incredible joy bursts forth within us as we
keep on celebrating our hope of experiencing God's glory!*

ROMANS 5:2 TPT

Let today's verse be a powerful encouragement to your heart, especially
knowing your faith opens doors that nothing else can. Your *yes* to Jesus
gives you permanent access to God. His grace and kindness are always
available. When you need strength for the battle, it will be given. When
you need peace through the process, it's yours for asking. When you need
hope, perspective, or wisdom, God will fill you with it.

No other relationship promises such things. Nothing on earth can
meet these kinds of needs. As a believer, you can continually delight in
God's goodness. You can rejoice in the truth that He will pour generosity
on those who choose to follow Him. So grab hold of your faith and the
beautiful benefits that come with it, and let it rise up as you trust in God.

Father, what a gift to know that as a believer in Jesus
I have permanent access to You. Birth in me a desire
to jump in with both feet and experience all faith has
to offer. I'm grateful You have made a way for me to
be close to You! In Jesus' name I pray. Amen.

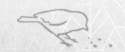

Stay on Guard

Most importantly, be disciplined and stay on guard. Your enemy
the devil is prowling around outside like a roaring lion, just
waiting and hoping for the chance to devour someone. Resist
him and be strong in your faith, knowing that your brothers and
sisters throughout the world are fellow sufferers with you.

1 PETER 5:8–9 VOICE

It's vital you stay on guard every day, making sure the enemy's plans
to take you out don't succeed. This instruction isn't a call to be stressed
out and worried. God isn't expecting you to exhaust yourself or become
paranoid. But He does want you to be aware that the enemy is real and
intends to hurt you. Consider the visual of the devil walking the perimeter
of your life looking for a way in. Where would the crack be? In what
area is your faith lacking?

Ask the Lord to strengthen you as you trust Him. With His help,
you'll be able to withstand any attacks because your borders will be
fortified by faith. Resisting the devil's tricks and traps will take discipline
and intentionality, but as you look to God as your source, you will find
all the strength you need.

Father, give me eyes to see and ears to hear when the enemy is
close. And give me courage to resist him as I stand strong in my
faith, trusting You. I know with Your help, I'll remain free from
anything the enemy throws my way. In Jesus' name I pray. Amen.

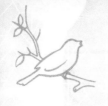

Not Worthy to Be Compared

For I consider that the sufferings of this present time are not worthy to be compared with the glory which shall be revealed in us.

ROMANS 8:18 NKJV

Life has a special way of punching us right in the gut, doesn't it? Often when we least expect it, a curveball comes out of nowhere. It may be a call from the doctor's office with unexpected test results. Maybe it's a note sent home about your child's behavior. It might be something inappropriate found on your husband's computer. Whatever it is, it unravels your sense of security, ignites panic, and leads to suffering.

In these moments, let your faith be what provides much-needed perspective. Scripture tells us that no matter how bad things are here on earth, they won't be worthy enough to be compared to the glory that will soon be revealed in us. The Greek word for "glory" is *doxa* and can also be translated "radiant beauty, splendor, perfection." That's quite a contrast to suffering, wouldn't you say? So keep focused on the doxa that's coming. You can access it through your faith.

Father, train my perspective to be anchored in Your glory rather than my present suffering. I know this life is but a breath, which means so are these tough seasons. Help my faith grow deep roots as I journey through the ups and downs of life. In Jesus' name I pray. Amen.

Work Together for Good

And we know that all things work together for good to those who love God, to those who are the called according to His purpose.

ROMANS 8:28 NKJV

It takes faith to believe today's key verse. Why? Because sometimes it's hard to wrap our head around how a divorce can be used for good. How can difficult and tragic events—a divorce, the death of a loved one, a bankruptcy, a serious illness—work together for good? But in God's economy, they do. As a matter of fact, we're told those who have faith will see *all things* act in concert together. . .and the Lord will bring good from them.

God promises to take events the enemy means for destruction and rework them. It's the concept of beauty from ashes (Isaiah 61:3). And it's a powerful promise that ensures pain has a point. When our faith rises up, we will have a unique perspective on the troubles we've faced. We'll be able to see how God has worked all difficult things together and the result was *good*.

Father, I don't understand how You'll manage to bring beauty from these ashes, but I know You will. While I may not always comprehend Your will and ways, I choose to have faith. I believe You. I trust You. And I am grateful for Your care and provision in my life. In Jesus' name I pray. Amen.

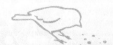

Purpose in the Storm

After you have suffered for a little while, the God of grace who has called you [to His everlasting presence] through Jesus the Anointed will restore you, support you, strengthen you, and ground you.

1 PETER 5:10 VOICE

Have faith and be strong! The suffering you're feeling right now is not forever. Like everything else, this season will pass when God ordains it. And when it's time—after you've felt the heat just long enough—He will intervene. The Lord will be faithful to restore you. He'll offer you His support. He'll provide the strength you need to get back on your feet. And He will set you on a solid foundation.

The truth is there are valuable lessons we can learn only in the storm. Often in times of trouble, God delivers gold nuggets of truth we can't get anywhere else. And this is where we realize the Lord is our source. What a beautiful revelation! Rather than expect the world to save us, we learn through suffering that God will meet any and every need— from food to finances to friendship. And through suffering we'll see our faith grow deep and wide.

Father, I'm listening. I'm watching. And I'm desperate for some relief. Show me Your goodness in the storms I am facing right now. Strengthen my faith and prove to be my source. I need You. In Jesus' name I pray. Amen.

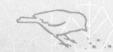

The Benefits of Troubled Times

Even in times of trouble we have a joyful confidence,
knowing that our pressures will develop in us patient endurance.
And patient endurance will refine our character, and proven
character leads us back to hope. And this hope is not a disappointing
fantasy, because we can now experience the endless love of God
cascading into our hearts through the Holy Spirit who lives in us!

ROMANS 5:3–5 TPT

When we read about the benefits that arise from times of trouble, they feel counterintuitive. We think hard times breed hard times. We decide suffering only brings more suffering. And when we think about seasons of struggling, we determine they only lead to more. How, then, can we expect to find joyful confidence, patient endurance, a refining of character, and hope as we battle? Faith.

These should be the times we are on our knees crying out to God for help. These are the times our prayers should be a continual conversation throughout each day. And these are also the times we will feel unexplainable peace as we rely on the Lord to sustain us. Let your faith rise up!

Father, how do You do it? How do You bring such goodness through my messy moments? Train my heart to hold on to You when times of trouble hit, trusting Your plans are bigger and better than I can ever imagine. In Jesus' name I pray. Amen.

A Faith-Builder

*Jesus went on to do many more miraculous signs in the presence
of his disciples, which are not even included in this book. But all
that is recorded here is so that you will fully believe that Jesus is
the Anointed One, the Son of God, and that through your faith in
him you will experience eternal life by the power of his name!*

JOHN 20:30–31 TPT

The Bible is an extremely important tool for your faith. Why? Because God specifically included in its pages stories and insights designed to grow your belief. It will encourage you to trust the Lord as you read of the times He came through. When the scriptures unpack God's sovereignty, you will find hope. And you will understand the depth and breadth of His love by digging into the story of Jesus' death and how it bridged the gap of sin.

Friend, He recorded it all for your benefit. He breathed His words onto the pages of the Bible through the hands of obedient men. And it was all for you, His beloved. Recognizing its divine inspiration, let God's Word be a treasure and a faith-builder in your life.

Father, thank You for telling Your story through the Bible.
What a powerful tool to grow my faith and encourage me
on my journey. Make it come alive as I read it, and use it
to strengthen my heart. In Jesus' name I pray. Amen.

A Reward for Waiting

But those who wait on the LORD shall renew their strength;
they shall mount up with wings like eagles, they shall run
and not be weary, they shall walk and not faint.

ISAIAH 40:31 NKJV

One of the most difficult parts of walking out our faith is learning to wait on the Lord. We live in a microwave society where we're used to getting what we want immediately. We complain about lines at the coffeehouse. We grow frustrated with being placed on hold. We can qualify for instant credit so we can buy the object of desire right then and there. We've been trained to expect instantaneous results.

God must have known impatience would be an issue, because He connects a reward with our waiting. We're told that if we activate our faith and wait patiently for His hand to move, our strength will be replenished. And that strength will furnish us with endurance for the battles ahead. It will give us perseverance to weather the storms. Let your faith rise up!

Father, give me the ability to wait on You to move in my situation. I don't want to rush Your timing or decide to take things into my own hands. Instead, I want to be patient and trust that You are working on my behalf. I will welcome the renewed strength You provide. In Jesus' name I pray. Amen.

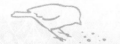

Faith Out Loud

"Stand up for me among the people you meet and the Son of Man will stand up for you before all God's angels. But if you pretend you don't know me, do you think I'll defend you before God's angels?"

LUKE 12:8–9 MSG

If you keep your faith tucked away and out of sight from those around you, others might wonder if you're really in a right relationship with God. If good works don't flow out of your time with the Lord, have you truly accepted Him as your Savior? Your belief in God should compel you to share Him with others. It should encourage you to speak up and speak out for Him. You should want your words and actions to point others to the Father. And when you stand up for His Son on earth, Jesus will stand up for you in the heavenlies.

How open are you with your faith? Do you promote God's saving power or hide your beliefs? Do you share your faith or keep it shut away? It's not about being obnoxious and over the top; it's about boasting in the Lord when the opportunity arises.

Father, I don't want my faith to be small. I don't want others to wonder if I am a follower of You. Please give me the courage to speak up when the door opens, lovingly and boldly. You are worthy to be praised, and I am humbled to be called a child of God. In Jesus' name I pray. Amen.

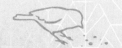

When You Struggle with Doubt

Then, looking into Thomas' eyes, he said, "Put your finger here in the wounds of my hands. Here—put your hand into my wounded side and see for yourself. Thomas, don't give in to your doubts any longer, just believe!" Then the words spilled out of his heart—"You are my Lord, and you are my God!"

JOHN 20:27–28 TPT

God knows exactly what you need to overcome doubts so your faith can grow and mature. He sees the mental and emotional barriers that keep you from going all in. And because of His infinite love for you, God will find a way to meet you right where you are. Remember, His heart for you is always good.

So what are your doubts? What keeps you from fully embracing faith? Maybe you're scared to get hurt again. Maybe you can't seem to trust anyone but yourself with an unknown future. Or maybe the idea of God and Jesus feels fantastical. Tell Him about your doubts and ask the Lord to speak into that specific area and replace your uncertainty with faith.

Father, I confess I struggle with doubt. Sometimes things just don't make sense to me and I can't take that leap of faith. Would You help me know the truth deep in my heart so I won't spend my time questioning? Meet me right here and help me believe. In Jesus' name I pray. Amen.

We Don't Need to See Him

You never saw him, yet you love him. You still don't see him,
yet you trust him—with laughter and singing. Because you kept on
believing, you'll get what you're looking forward to: total salvation.

1 PETER 1:8–9 MSG

Faith is a choice. It's choosing to trust in a person or a thing to do what it is supposed to do. You trust a chair to hold your weight. You have faith that your garage door opener will work. You believe that when you turn off the oven, it will in fact turn off. And why do we have faith in things like this? Because they have proven to be true over and over again.

When we place our faith in the Lord, we don't have to see Him first. We don't have to touch Him. God is able to turn our heart toward Him so we can believe blindly. But our faith grows by seeing His fingerprints in our life. It matures by trusting Him with our heart. And as we spend more time with God, the Holy Spirit bonds us together.

Father, I've never seen You, but I deeply love You. I've
never physically felt Your hug of comfort, but I've been
comforted by You. And I know my faith is what allows me
to trust that You are alive and active in my life. Thank You
for being with me always. In Jesus' name I pray. Amen.

The New Shape of Life

Oh, the joys of those who do not follow evil men's advice, who do not hang around with sinners, scoffing at the things of God. But they delight in doing everything God wants them to, and day and night are always meditating on his laws and thinking about ways to follow him more closely.

PSALM 1:1–2 TLB

When you become a believer, your life should begin to take on a new shape. It may be a slow transformation, or it could be instantaneous. Some areas may change fast while others need more intentionality. And no two people's experiences are the same. Your faith is a very personal process between you and God. But make no mistake—change must happen.

You'll have a desire to follow God's plan and get to know Him more deeply. You will feel the Holy Spirit's gut check pointing you in a certain direction when you need to make a difficult decision. You'll yearn to step out of sinful patterns and make better choices with your life. And little by little, your faith will deepen its roots and grow into something beautiful.

Father, mature my faith so I can experience Your goodness every day. Let me seek You as I navigate the changes a life of belief brings. Make me ready to have You reshape my life. I trust You to bring about the changes that need to happen. In Jesus' name I pray. Amen.

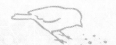

Drenched in Prayer

Don't be pulled in different directions or worried about a thing.
Be saturated in prayer throughout each day, offering your faith-filled
requests before God with overflowing gratitude. Tell him every
detail of your life, then God's wonderful peace that transcends human
understanding, will guard your heart and mind through Jesus Christ.

PHILIPPIANS 4:6–7 TPT

Without a doubt, the greatest antidote to the weight of worry you're carrying on your shoulders is prayer. When you're overwhelmed by anxiety and unable to focus on what matters, go directly to God. The Word says to be saturated in prayer—drenched in it—asking the Lord for what you need and being full of thanksgiving. The truth is He wants to hear you share every detail of your situation. Of course He's already fully aware, but God delights in those times of community with you, His beloved.

Let your faith drive you to your Father in heaven. He is the only One who can understand the complexity of the emotions you're feeling. And in return, God will pass on His peace, the kind the world can never emulate.

Father, I want to be in constant communication with
You. I don't need a specific time or place to open up
and share my worries. Instead, remind me to go straight
to You in moments of turmoil, trusting You'll calm my
anxious heart. I'm so grateful I can talk directly to You
anytime and anywhere! In Jesus' name I pray. Amen.

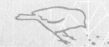

Part of the Process or Part of the Problem?

What we read in Scripture is, "Abraham entered into what God was doing for him, and that was the turning point. He trusted God to set him right instead of trying to be right on his own."

ROMANS 4:3 MSG

Your life will be so much better when you choose to be part of the process rather than part of the problem. Either you can enter into what God is doing in your life, or you can fight against it. You can embrace change or buck the system. Of course the Lord wants you to partner with Him, following His will and ways, but you always have a choice.

Did you notice in today's verse that when Abraham joined in with God's work in his life, he came to an important turning point? A shift occurred in his thinking. Instead of being set in his ways, Abraham trusted God to set him right. He surrendered his need to be in control. And it made all the difference. Do you have the faith to be part of the process rather than part of the problem?

Father, deepen my faith so I am able to trust Your will for my life. Let me surrender my ideas and plans in exchange for Yours. Let me follow Your leading in all things. I want to be part of Your process. In Jesus' name I pray. Amen.

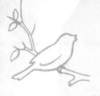

Who Is God to You?

He's the hope that holds me and the stronghold to shelter me,
the only God for me, and my great confidence. He will
rescue you from every hidden trap of the enemy, and he will
protect you from false accusation and any deadly curse.

PSALM 91:2–3 TPT

What a massive promise in this passage of scripture from Psalm 91. The author has a clear vision of who God is in his life. His faith is strong and unshakable. He knows his hope and stronghold are in the Lord, who provides perfect shelter. He is why the psalmist can have confidence. Because God knows every hidden trap, the psalmist can depend on being saved from them. Even more, he can trust that anything false that comes against him will be demolished.

Who is God to you, friend? Where have you seen Him working in your life? What do you believe about Him? Take time today to think through these questions, and then write out a statement of your faith. Share it with God, asking Him to speak into it. Have a clear vision of who God is in *your* life.

Father, help me have an accurate understanding of who You
are in my life. Help me know the truth or learn the real truth.
I never want to diminish You or Your goodness. Instead, open
my eyes to all the ways You've been active in the circumstances
I've had to face. Grow my faith! In Jesus' name I pray. Amen.

When Scripture Doesn't Feel True for You

Like a bird protecting its young, God will cover you with His
feathers, will protect you under His great wings; His faithfulness
will form a shield around you, a rock-solid wall to protect you.

PSALM 91:4 VOICE

You may read today's verse and scoff because you feel anything but protected by God. Reading about being covered and shielded makes you sad because you can't relate. It doesn't feel familiar. Maybe it has never seemed as if anyone was looking out for you, much less the Lord. So you struggle with these sections of scripture.

It has been said we'd be blown away by all we *have* been saved from—situations we were never aware of. The truth is everything that comes into our life has been approved by God. And He only allows hard things because they're for our benefit and His glory. They are approved and limited, according to His will. Ask God to speak into any feelings of rejection or abandonment. And ask for the faith to believe the truth.

Father, it's hard for me to believe I've been held by You
because I've been through so much trauma. I need the Holy
Spirit to whisper into my heart what is true. I need my
eyes to be opened to the truth. And I need You to help me
believe the parts of Your Word that don't seem to apply to
me. Help my unbelief, Lord! In Jesus' name I pray. Amen.

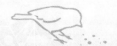

Protected and Guarded

He will command His heavenly messengers to guard you, to keep you safe in every way. They will hold you up in their hands so that you will not crash, or fall, or even graze your foot on a stone. You will walk on the lion and the cobra; you will trample the lion and the serpent underfoot.

PSALM 91:11–13 VOICE

Don't worry. That directive is often easier said than done, but the idea is based on God's promise of protection from His Word. It takes faith to trust He will save you from harm, especially when it surrounds you on all sides. But today's scripture says He will keep you safe in every way.

Please don't think that means you won't face hard seasons. You will struggle in relationships. Your finances will be squeezed at times. You'll face countless challenges that will threaten your confidence and cause heartache. But God has commanded you to be protected, and so you will, according to His plan. Have the faith to trust He has your back.

Father, help me have faith to believe You'll protect me. But let me also know it may not match up with my idea of protection. In this life I will have trouble, but I can trust You to be with me in it. Let my heart become light as I accept Your will and ways for my future. In Jesus' name I pray. Amen.

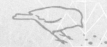

Believing God's Word

*In the beginning, God created everything: the heavens above
and the earth below. Here's what happened: At first the earth
lacked shape and was totally empty, and a dark fog draped
over the deep while God's spirit-wind hovered over the
surface of the empty waters. Then there was the voice of God.*

GENESIS 1:1–2 VOICE

God created everything. From the heavens to the earth, the land to the sea, the plant life to the animals, to His deeply cherished possession, humankind, creation was orchestrated by the Lord. Some may think the scriptures that unpack history are too fantastical. They might argue over the length of time creation actually took. Some may believe there was a big bang that formed our planet. But if we are going to be women of faith, then we take God at His Word. All of it.

If God says He created everything, then by faith we believe it to be true. The Lord is sovereign, and He has no equal. And if we were to take an honest look at our life, we'd see a perfect track record of God being who He says He is.

Father, I choose to believe Your Word to be true in every way.
Help me hold on to this belief even when the world tries to sway
my opinion. Give me courage to stand my ground as I give You
the glory for every good thing. In Jesus' name I pray. Amen.

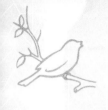

The Connection between Faith and Works

Go ahead then and prove to me that you have faith without works and I will show you faith by my works as proof that I believe. You can believe all you want that there is one true God, that's wonderful! But even the demons know this and tremble with fear before him, yet they're unchanged—they remain demons.

JAMES 2:18–19 TPT

Doing good things will not ensure an eternity in heaven. Bringing a meal to a needy family, cleaning someone's home, volunteering at a local charity, and donating clothes to a woman's shelter are all wonderful acts of kindness, but they won't open the pearly gates for you once you die. What they do, however, is offer a tangible example of your changed heart. They are outward expressions of your faith.

Scripture says good works and faith go hand in hand. We secure eternity by believing Jesus is the Son of God who died for our sins and rose three days later. We do nothing to be saved other than choose to believe. And then our heart, transformed by our faith, prompts us to do good works that point to God above. The two can't be separated.

Father, change my heart through faith so it shows
through my actions. Let them be proof that I
believe in You. In Jesus' name I pray. Amen.

The Call to Love

Your calling is to fulfill the royal law of love as given to us in this
Scripture: "You must love and value your neighbor as you love and value
yourself!" For keeping this law is the noble way to live. But when you
show prejudice you commit sin and you violate this royal law of love!

JAMES 2:8–9 TPT

We all have specific callings on our lives designed to further the message of Jesus. Yours may be to preach or teach. It may be to write books. Maybe it's to be a missionary or be in a worship band. When God created you, He determined a beautiful purpose for your life. What is yours?

But while we all have different callings, there is one that unites us together. There is one that knits everyone in faith. And that calling is to love. Love is the royal law we're to follow. Not only are we to love ourselves (which is sometimes hard to do), but we're also to love others. Even more, it's not our job to determine who is worthy of our love and who isn't. Empowered by God through our faith, we're simply to love earnestly and sincerely.

Father, the call to love is a tough one because there are
some people I don't want to love, and You know why. But
now I understand it is Your law and I feel convicted. Soften
my heart and make it tender toward others. And give me
courage to choose the high road. In Jesus' name I pray. Amen.

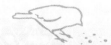

Disciplined Because of Love

And have you forgotten his encouraging words spoken to you as his children? He said, "My child, don't underestimate the value of the discipline and training of the Lord God, or get depressed when he has to correct you. For the Lord's training of your life is the evidence of his faithful love. And when he draws you to himself, it proves you are his delightful child."

HEBREWS 12:5–6 TPT

Let's be honest. No one likes to be disciplined—not as a child and especially not as an adult. We don't like to be told we've fallen short. We despise any kind of criticism, even the constructive kind. Life has a special way of beating us up already, so why would we want to hear negativity from someone else?

Just as we want the very best for our kids, so does God. He wants to guide and direct us to stay on the right path, and often that means He must course-correct us when we start to veer off. It's because God loves and cares for you that He is quick to correct—just as we are quick to correct our own kids. Determine to view the Lord's discipline as evidence of His faithful love rather than a hurtful slap on the wrist that causes us to pull back from Him.

Father, help me trust that Your correction is based in love and not disappointment. In Jesus' name I pray. Amen.

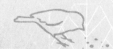

What to Do with Fear

But when I am afraid, I will put my confidence in you.
Yes, I will trust the promises of God. And since I am
trusting him, what can mere man do to me?

PSALM 56:3–4 TLB

What scares you? What stirs up your emotions and gives you a sense of dread? Maybe it's fear you'll never find a husband. Maybe it's that you'll never be a mother, something you've wanted for so long. Is your fear connected to your finances or your health? Are you a chronic worrier, often predicting horrible outcomes and endings for your own or your kids' futures? Maybe your fear is connected to losing someone you love or never finding your own happiness. Or maybe you are terrified of exposing your heart to another and getting hurt. . .*again.*

One of the beautiful gifts that comes with your faith in God is peace. It's that feeling that washes over you that can't be matched by anything worldly. It's confidence that the Lord is working so you don't have to. It's the surrender of your fears and insecurities and a trust in God to right every wrong. Be quick to grab onto Him when anxiety creeps in. He's got you.

> Father, You know what's swirling in my heart
> and how it's making me feel. You understand the
> intricacies of my emotions. I'm putting my confidence
> in You and anchoring my faith in Your promises. I know
> You won't disappoint! In Jesus' name I pray. Amen.

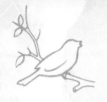

You Are Heard

At that time, you will call out for Me, and I will hear.
You will pray, and I will listen. You will look for
Me intently, and you will find Me.

JEREMIAH 29:12–13 VOICE

Do you ever feel as if your prayers bounce off the ceiling and land flat on the floor? Does it seem like God isn't listening to you because you're not seeing the results you want? Are you beginning to question if He even has the time to focus on you and your needs? If so, ask God to reveal if there is unconfessed sin in your life. Ask Him to uncover whatever may be a block in your relationship. Sometimes we get weary in our faith because we don't feel we're as connected to God as we want to be. Ask Him about it.

But be confident that when you are in a right relationship with Him, you are heard. When you cry out, when you pray for God's help, He hears you and promises to listen. God doesn't hide. When you lift your voice to the Lord—be it in sorrow, tribulation, or gratitude—His focus is fully on your words. It takes faith to pray to Someone you cannot see or touch, but have confidence God is real and really loves you. And when you seek Him with intentionality, you will find Him.

Father, show me anything that may be blocking my
relationship with You. In Jesus' name I pray. Amen.

Noticed and Collected

You have seen me tossing and turning through the night.
You have collected all my tears and preserved them in your
bottle! You have recorded every one in your book.

PSALM 56:8 TLB

Think of the times your worries and concerns caused sleepless nights. You stayed awake mulling things over, unable to calm yourself down. Even worse, no one was there to help. And recall the painful moments that caused an overflow of tears to spill from your eyes—liquid words you were unable to share with others. Remember the seasons of loss and grief when your heart was breaking and all you could do was weep, unable to be consoled. God remembers them too.

Scripture tells us that every restless night and every shed tear was noticed and recorded. While we may have felt alone in those moments, unseen and uncared for, we were not. God was right there with us. And because He has promised never to leave us nor forsake us, we can have faith He'll be there every time we're struggling.

Father, I take great comfort in the realization that You've been with me through the tears and the sleeplessness. Those were painful times to navigate. Thank You for caring enough not to leave me alone. The revelation of Your nearness blesses me! And my heart is full knowing You'll be with me the next time I face hardship too. In Jesus' name I pray. Amen.

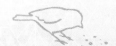

Let God In

Open up before God, *keep nothing back; he'll do*
whatever needs to be done: He'll validate your life in the
clear light of day and stamp you with approval at high noon.

PSALM 37:5–6 MSG

So many of us live guarded lives. We keep our true feelings and emotions close to the vest and project to others the life we want them to see. We post images and updates on social media that show a snapshot of a perfect life—a life nothing close to our reality. Our faces shine with bright and cheery smiles, but all the while we're hoping the truth of how we're actually feeling stays concealed. Why do we hide our hearts this way?

God already knows the complexity of what you're trying to tuck away. He knows the depths of your heart better than you do. He understands in great detail what you're feeling and why you don't want others to know. And, friend, He longs for you to open up before Him and share your pain. God wants to hear your heart. Let Him in and ask for what you need. Let Him be your safe space.

Father, mature my faith so I can trust You with my heart.
I've hidden it for so long that it's hard to let anyone in again.
Build my confidence in Your desire to see the real me, and
gently draw me closer to You. In Jesus' name I pray. Amen.

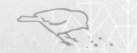

The God Who Saves and Steadies

For You have saved my soul from the darkness of death,
steadied my feet from stumbling so I might continue to
walk before God, embraced in the light of the living.

PSALM 56:13 VOICE

God is a God who saves and steadies. Chances are you've seen His rescuing power in your own life. Maybe He saved you from the death of a marriage. Maybe it was from financial ruin. Did He resuscitate your broken heart after a tough season of parenting? Has He saved you from the pit of despair after the loss of someone you deeply loved? Maybe He set your feet on a firm foundation after a relational disaster or held you steady during a tumultuous season of illness.

Let your faith in God deepen its roots as you watch Him intervene in your life. Let your front row seat to His goodness be what anchors your heart to His. Decide to trust in God's power and strength more than anything else. What an amazing God we have the privilege to serve! Embrace this time on earth and let your faith rise!

Father, as I look back at my crazy life, I can see the times
You were the One to save and steady me. I'm so grateful
for Your deliverance, and I give You the glory. Allow me to
see Your intervention clearly so I can point others to Your
goodness and faithfulness. In Jesus' name I pray. Amen.

Who Speaks into Your Life?

God-lovers make the best counselors. Their words possess wisdom
and are right and trustworthy. The ways of God are in their hearts
and they won't swerve from the paths of steadfast righteousness.

PSALM 37:30–31 TPT

Be careful about who you allow to speak into your life. The reality is that not every person believes like you do. They may not be in a saving relationship with Jesus. They may never open the Bible or believe it is God's inspired Word. They may have a skewed understanding of the Lord and His sovereignty. Protecting your mind from bad counsel is vital. You must be vigilant about guarding your heart from ungodly advice.

So think about it. Whose opinion matters to you? Who do you go to for guidance and instruction? A parent? Aunt? Small group leader? Mentor? Friend? Are they rooted in their faith, and do they challenge you to be the same? Do they walk the walk, living out the counsel they share? Ask the Lord to help you discern who is trustworthy and faith-filled, as well as those whose good intentions might steer you in the wrong direction.

Father, help me make wise choices as I seek out counselors to speak into my life. I know I need to be shrewd because bad counsel can lead me down wrong paths. And remind me to listen for Your confirmation in the advice given to me, making sure I am on the right track. In Jesus' name I pray. Amen.

The Nudge to Notice

Never walk away from someone who deserves help; your hand is
God's *hand for that person. Don't tell your neighbor "Maybe some*
other time" or "Try me tomorrow" when the money's right there
in your pocket. Don't figure ways of taking advantage of your
neighbor when he's sitting there trusting and unsuspecting.

PROVERBS 3:27–29 MSG

Part of living a faithful life is loving and caring for others. We have
to be alert to the Holy Spirit's prompting, realizing He often gives us
nudges to notice the needs of others. Too often we're so wrapped up in
the problems and challenges of the day that we fail to see when someone else is lacking. In our desire to stay comfortable, we can be stingy
with our time and treasure. Yet we should have respect for those around
us and resolve to live in harmony and community.

Think of someone who stood in the gap for you in a time of need.
Remember seasons when people circled the wagons to support you or
your family. Maybe you've experienced generosity on unexpected levels
that left a mark on your heart. In faith, follow God's lead to love on the
ones He has placed in your path.

Father, open my eyes to see the needs of others, and grow
in me Your generous spirit so I am moved to help however
I can. My heart is open to where You lead me. Let me be
Your hands and feet. In Jesus' name I pray. Amen.

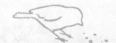

He Will Lift Your Chin

I'm hurting, Lord—will you forget me forever? How much longer, Lord? Will you look the other way when I'm in need? How much longer must I cling to this constant grief? I've endured this shaking of my soul. So how much longer will my enemy have the upper hand?

PSALM 13:1–2 TPT

Have you ever felt the way the psalmist is feeling in today's verse? When life feels overwhelming, sometimes we feel like we're underwater. We experience the weight of worry and the saturation of stress. And even worse, sometimes we feel like we're all alone in the depths. Feeling abandoned by friends and family is bad enough. But feeling left behind by God can push us into despair.

When a sense of despair threatens to overtake your thoughts, returning to the Bible is vitally important. Doing so will not only encourage you but also remind you of the truth that God will never leave you or forsake you. These desperate moments are best spent in His presence for reassurance. In Him is where you will find peace. Time with Him is what will strengthen your faith. In moments of quiet communion the Lord will meet you and lift your chin with hope.

Father, I don't like feeling rejected or abandoned. I don't like feeling unheard. I don't like feeling unimportant. Speak truth into my weary soul and remind me that I am loved. And please help me rise from the depths. In Jesus' name I pray. Amen.

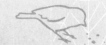

Celebrate the Rescue

*I've thrown myself headlong into your arms—I'm celebrating your rescue.
I'm singing at the top of my lungs, I'm so full of answered prayers.*

PSALM 13:5–6 MSG

How many times have we overlooked the rescue and simply moved on rather than taking a moment to realize what just happened? When the marriage was restored from the brink of divorce, we let out a sigh of relief and moved forward. When the treatment worked and the doctor gave a clean bill of health, we exhaled and then moved on to the next issue. When the error was fixed and our credit restored, we simply crossed it off the to-do list.

Why don't we celebrate God's hand in our situation? What keeps us from taking a moment to give Him the glory? The psalmist's response leaves nothing to the imagination. We know exactly what he felt. He threw himself into the arms of God with thanksgiving, recognizing and singing about His goodness. When it comes to celebrating what God has done, let's not be dismissive or subdued. Instead, let faith rise as we lift our hands in praise to the Lord!

Father, forgive me for the times I haven't properly celebrated
the ways You've rescued me. I see Your hand now and then,
and I am full of gratitude! I'm singing Your praises—I'm giving
You the glory, Lord! You are the One who rescues, and I'm so
thankful for Your boundless love! In Jesus' name I pray. Amen.

When Bullies Strike

Don't walk around with a chip on your shoulder, always
spoiling for a fight. Don't try to be like those who shoulder their way
through life. Why be a bully? "Why not?" you say. Because GOD can't
stand twisted souls. It's the straightforward who get his respect.

PROVERBS 3:30–32 MSG

No one likes a bully. We don't like it when someone pushes us around or tries to make us feel bad about ourselves. Why is it that what makes us different is so often the catalyst for mean-spiritedness? Didn't God make us unique? Aren't we one-of-a-kind by design? It's hard enough to find the courage to like yourself without someone pointing out flaws.

God doesn't like a bully attitude either. You were made on purpose, and He doesn't want His beloved to be devalued by others. Because your faith gives you direct access to God, take your feelings of being "less than" straight to Him. Let the Lord remind you of why you're important. Let Him speak the truth of who you are. And ask for the faith to believe Him more than any naysayer.

Father, I've been the victim of a bully who made me feel insignificant. They said cruel words that made me doubt my worth. They made me question my value as a woman. And I remember the discouragement I felt as a result. Let me be quick to run to You for the truth rather than subscribe to their lies again. In Jesus' name I pray. Amen.

The Pursuit of Peace

You will keep the peace, a perfect peace, for all who trust in You,
for those who dedicate their hearts and minds to You. So
trust in the Eternal One forever, for He is like a great
Rock—strong, stable, trustworthy, and lasting.

ISAIAH 26:3–4 VOICE

When you put your faith in God, scripture says you'll receive a perfect peace. You'll experience an unmatched sense of calm in the middle of the storms. Your willingness to trust His will and ways will bless you. And He will bring stability to you and the situations that rock you.

The truth is, no earthly remedy can outperform or outlast the peace of God. And it's not like we haven't tried to find such a remedy, right? Think of all the ways you have pursued peace. Ignoring the situation. Retail therapy. Netflix binging. Meditation or yoga. Self-help books and seminars. And while these may have helped for a minute, you were soon back in chaos. Let your faith rise above it all and trust God with every burden.

Father, would You please settle my spirit? I'm stressed
and worried and full of anxiety, and I know You are
the only One who can give me the perfect peace I'm
looking for. Thank You for being trustworthy and faithful.
I realize You are all I need. In Jesus' name I pray. Amen.

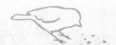

The Faith to Endure and Persevere

I waited and waited and waited some more, patiently, knowing God would come through for me. Then, at last, he bent down and listened to my cry. He stooped down to lift me out of danger from the desolate pit I was in, out of the muddy mess I had fallen into. Now he's lifted me up into a firm, secure place and steadied me while I walk along his ascending path.

PSALM 40:1–2 TPT

As your faith matures, so does your ability to endure and persevere. Why? Because you develop the ability to trust that God is working in your situation. You learn to believe your unknown future is safe and secure with a known God. You grab onto the peace that faith affords you. And you begin to see life from an eternal perspective, trusting the Lord's timing and plan over what you see in the natural.

God won't let you down. He will not leave you and promises never to forsake you. He may not work on your timeline or in the ways you want, but God's will and ways are perfect. Have faith in Him.

Father, I will wait until You choose to move in my situation. I know You see me and Your heart for me is good. Give me the faith to stand firm in those truths. In Jesus' name I pray. Amen.

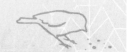

Faith Is Fun!

*I'm whistling, laughing, and jumping for joy; I'm singing
your song, High God. The day my enemies turned tail and ran,
they stumbled on you and fell on their faces. You took over and set
everything right; when I needed you, you were there, taking charge.*

PSALM 9:2–4 MSG

Faith can be hard to walk out because it requires huge amounts of grit
and grace. It can challenge you on every level, especially when you need it
the most. But faith can also be loads of fun as you partner with God each
day! Watching Him make right from wrong or good from bad is cause
for celebration! Witnessing His kindness in deliverance puts a smile on
your face. Seeing God meet your needs one by one makes you jump for
joy. And when you discover the ways He has protected you from your
enemies, you just might fall over in laughter.

God will always be there when you need Him. He's not too busy
or fed up with your requests. You don't ask too much, nor are you high
maintenance. God is just and fair, and He loves you fully and completely.
Know He will always lead from that position.

Father, there are too many benefits to count for anchoring
my faith in You. But along with so many other things, life
with You is fun! Grow my trust in Your goodness so I can live
out every benefit, every day. In Jesus' name I pray. Amen.

Just a Little Longer

And now, O Lord, have mercy on me; see how I suffer at the hands of those who hate me. Lord, snatch me back from the jaws of death. Save me, so that I can praise you publicly before all the people at Jerusalem's gates and rejoice that you have rescued me.

PSALM 9:13–14 TLB

Hold on a little longer, friend. You may be at the end of your rope, but hold on. You may be on your last leg, but keep standing. You may be eyeball-deep in worry and stress, but keep blinking. Remember that God is never early and never late. He knows the exact moment to make an entrance onto the scene and snatch you from the jaws of death. Your job is to have steadfast faith, trusting He has full knowledge and is working out every detail.

And when He does—because He will—be loud about it. Give God the glory. Point to Him with your words and actions. Let there be no doubt who just saved you. Who knows—maybe He'll use that situation to win a heart and secure someone's salvation. And your faith will have played a part in it.

Father, give me the courage to hold on a little longer.
In those moments when I want to give up and give
in, remind me that You will always be there to rescue
and restore. In Jesus' name I pray. Amen.

Bragging on God

A new song for a new day rises up in me every time I think about
how he breaks through for me! Ecstatic praise pours out of my mouth
until everyone hears how God has set me free. Many will see his
miracles; they'll stand in awe of God and fall in love with him!

PSALM 40:3 TPT

Do you brag on God? Do you tell others about the ways He has honored your faith by releasing you from the bondage caused by fear? Have you ever opened up about times He helped you break through the lies of insecurity? What about when God detangled you from people who didn't have your best interests in mind? There's no doubt the Lord has worked miracles in your life to give you the freedom Jesus came to give.

So open your mouth and share them. Don't keep His goodness tucked away, because those around you need to hear it. Your testimony strengthens the faith of others and builds the hope God will show up for them too. Give Him your praises and celebrate His kindness and generosity with the people He has placed in your life!

Father, oh the number of times You have brought freedom into my life. Thank You for never giving up on me. Thank You for never being exhausted by me. And thank You for all the breakthrough moments—the ones no one could argue were only because of Your goodness. In Jesus' name I pray. Amen.

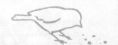

Expression of Love

O Lord, our God, no one can compare with you. Such wonderful works and miracles are all found with you! And you think of us all the time with your countless expressions of love—far exceeding our expectations!

PSALM 40:5 TPT

Scripture tells us that God demonstrates love for His children in ways too numerous to count. He does this because He can't get you off His mind. You're a constant thought. Let that sink in.

Think about the ways you've seen God work in your life. How has He shown adoration toward you in the past? Maybe you have a deep sense of the Lord's pleasure in your spirit. Have you seen His favor through answered prayers or open doors? Does He honor your faith with an unshakable sense of peace? Are you surrounded with amazing community to help you navigate life? Have you watched unfixable relationships be restored? Spend time today recognizing God's expressions of love, and thank Him for pouring them out onto you.

Father, when I take inventory of all the ways You've showed me your love, I am speechless. I confess I haven't always seen them, nor have I realized they had Your fingerprints all over them. But I know all good things come from You, and I'm so very grateful. You're an amazing Father, and I love You too! In Jesus' name I pray. Amen.

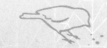

The Value of Community

Now may the God of patience and comfort grant you to be like-minded toward one another, according to Christ Jesus, that you may with one mind and one mouth glorify the God and Father of our Lord Jesus Christ.

ROMANS 15:5–6 NKJV

Community is important. As a matter of fact, God created us to need one another. Together we are powerful! Even introverts must leave their retreat centers from time to time because positive interaction with others is desired. God created us for relationships—both with Him and with those around us. United, we're capable of sharing faith with the masses. But community can also be tricky.

Since we're flawed humans surrounded by other flawed humans, doing life with others can be a setup for frustration. People we dearly love can also be the ones to get on our last nerve. We often struggle to see eye to eye or find common ground. That's why we need to ask God to knit our hearts together. It's why we ask Him to help us be like-minded so we can join together to make a meaningful impact for His kingdom while on earth. It's why we flex our faith and trust God to create the right kind of community in our lives.

Father, help me build a community of friends and family
to do day-to-day life with. I'm eager to be like-minded
with others, standing united as we proclaim Your glory
to anyone who will listen. In Jesus' name I pray. Amen.

The Fresh Air of Freedom

I will be found by you, says the LORD, and I will bring you back from your captivity; I will gather you from all the nations and from all the places where I have driven you, says the LORD, and I will bring you to the place from which I cause you to be carried away captive.

JEREMIAH 29:14 NKJV

Every time you cry out for help, seeking the Lord through the fog and fear, you'll find Him. Sometimes we believe God is some far-away, untouchable God who doesn't have time for us or any interest in what's going on down in our neck of the woods. We think that since we got ourselves into this mess, we have to find our own way out. We assume the bondage we're tangled in is punishment for bad choices. But faith tells us the Lord specializes in freeing captives and restoring them. So we ask Him.

Don't sit in your mess, defeated and joyless. Don't let fear or insecurity chain you to a life of hopelessness. God has deep compassion for His children who feel stuck. He makes a path out for those who feel trapped. So be quick to activate your faith every time you feel the wind of captivity blow your direction. Don't stand for it any longer, because God made a way to breathe the fresh air of freedom.

Father, thank You for the freedom I have through Jesus! In His name I pray. Amen.

Don't Let Messy Be Your Identity

And me? I'm a mess. I'm nothing and have nothing: make something of me. You can do it; you've got what it takes—but God, don't put it off.

PSALM 40:17 MSG

Many of us let being a mess be our identity. We almost wear our messiness with pride, quick to admit we're unsteady and struggling. Why? Because there's a payoff. It may be pity. It may be attention. Or it may be something else that makes it worthwhile in our mind. So rather than work through the issues to find resolution, we stay stuck in the strife and stress of life. We make peace with it. And we decide this is who we are and how our life will always be.

Rise above that mindset, friend. Your faith opens the door to live in victory, and that's where you want to be. The reality is that the victim mentality is terribly unattractive and completely self-serving. Instead, embrace the freedom God offers through Jesus. Just ask Him for it! There's no reason to sit in your mess one more minute, especially because joy is right around the corner.

Father, even if my life is a mess, that doesn't mean I'm a mess. When I take my brokenness to You, I'll be restored and renewed to live in victory! Keep me from seeing anything good about being a victim. It's not the kind of life I want to live! In Jesus' name I pray. Amen.

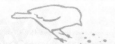

A Safe-House for the Battered

GOD's a safe-house for the battered, a sanctuary during bad times. The moment you arrive, you relax; you're never sorry you knocked.

PSALM 9:10 MSG

Where are you being battered these days? Where is life beating you up? Are you trying to parent a teenager who is making every wrong choice in the book? Is your business struggling financially and all your eggs are in this basket? Are you recently divorced and grieving the loss of the life you thought was real and true? Are you lacking meaningful community and dealing with deep loneliness? Is unwarranted criticism coming your way and you're not sure how to navigate it? Does bad news keep popping up?

There are a million ways the world promises to take care of you. There are thousands of options designed to make you feel better. Honestly, though, none of them work—at least not for long. But when you limp to the Lord, He will meet you and revive your weary heart. He is a safe-house and sanctuary, always open to those who love Him. Your faith in God brings the beautiful assurance of help.

Father, I have nothing to offer You but my heavy and broken heart. I've tried to heal myself but have failed. I've relied on others, but they've let me down. I should have run to You right from the start, for You are the safe-house and sanctuary I desperately need. Please help me. In Jesus' name I pray. Amen.

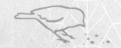

Radical Trust and Bold Confidence

Out of my deep anguish and pain I prayed, and God, you helped
me as a father. You came to my rescue and broke open the way
into a beautiful and broad place. Now I know, Lord, that you
are for me, and I will never fear what man can do to me.

PSALM 118:5–6 TPT

Isn't it amazing how God shows His love for us? Can you hear the relief in the psalmist's voice in today's scripture passage? Can you hear the genuine appreciation? Do you see the cause and effect? The psalmist prayed for help and God honored the request, just as any good and loving parent would do. And His response birthed a radical trust and a bold confidence in the writer.

Now think about your own life. Can you recall a time when you prayed to God with your soul crushed and your heart broken, and you felt the love of the Father settle over you? Have you watched Him make a way when you saw none before you? Let the Lord turn your heart toward Him with a fresh revelation of His love for you. And let that love grow your faith into radical trust and bold confidence in Him.

Father, I'm so grateful for the powerful ways You show Your
love. Use them to grow my faith in Your awesomeness as
I try to navigate this life. In Jesus' name I pray. Amen.

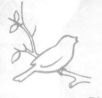

Surrounded by Trouble

Please, Eternal One, don't hold back Your kind ways from me.
I need Your strong love and truth to stand watch over me
and keep me from harm. Right now I can't see because I am
surrounded by troubles; my sins and shortcomings have caught
up to me, so I am swimming in darkness. Like the hairs on my
head, there are too many to count, so my heart deserts me.

PSALM 40:11–12 VOICE

Oh, what we would give to feel God's kindness blanket us when we are surrounded by trouble. To know He will love us through the mess and strengthen us for the battle is our desperate cry from the valleys of life. When we're overwhelmed by the troubles of life, we can feel alone and lost, an anxious place where only the Lord can bring a sense of calm. To feel protected in our weakness gives us a great sense of comfort, especially in our fearful and vulnerable state.

Go to God and ask Him to save you. Pour out your heart, sharing what you need in that moment. Ask for His kindness and gentleness to overshadow your circumstances. And ask all this in faith.

Father, these desperate moments are hard to walk out because
everything feels out of control. The weight of worry presses
down hard on my shoulders. I'm fraught and frantic, as if I'm
swimming in darkness. Please save me. Lift me out of this chaos
and set me on solid ground. In Jesus' name I pray. Amen.

God's Wisdom and Knowledge

*My son, never lose sight of God's wisdom and knowledge: make
decisions out of true wisdom, guard your good sense, and they will be life
to your soul and fine jewelry around your neck. Then each one of your steps
will land securely on your life's journey, and you will not trip or fall.*

PROVERBS 3:21–23 VOICE

God's wisdom and discernment are available to His beloved. Where we
hit the wall in our understanding of life's situations, He sees the whole
enchilada. He's aware of the ins and outs. And He knows exactly what
to do next. The ability to tap into God's knowledge is an unmatched
blessing we can access when we need it. And doing so is a beautiful
expression of our faith.

Where do you need His wisdom today? What are you trying to
navigate that feels above your paygrade? Maybe you're parenting a
special needs child. Maybe you're getting ready to take the next step
after discovering your husband's betrayal. Maybe you're helping a friend
walk through grief. Regardless, ask God—with thanksgiving—to fill
you with His discernment and knowledge.

Father, I don't know where to go from here. I'm not sure which
step forward is the right one. I long to understand the situation
at hand and make smart decisions in response to it. I know You'll
help me, and I'm so grateful You care! In Jesus' name I pray. Amen.

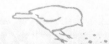

117

The Hero in Your Story

For you stand beside me as my hero who rescues me.
I've seen with my own eyes the defeat of my enemies. I've
triumphed over them all! Lord, it is so much better to trust
in you to save me than to put my confidence in someone else.

PSALM 118:7–8 TPT

One of the greatest ways our faith is restored or built up is by being able to witness God moving in our life. Sometimes we know our hands brought about a change. But then there are times we see something we know was only by the Lord's hands. We recognize it was accomplished by Him alone because we know it would have been impossible through human efforts. And in these miracle moments, we not only are humbled by His kindness but also gain confidence and trust in our God.

If you will trust Him enough to step aside, the Lord will be the hero of your story. He will do great things while you watch them happen. He's not a genie in a bottle, answering your commands. He cannot be manipulated. But when you understand the blessings that come from securing your faith in God, you will confidently trust His will and ways in your circumstances.

Father, open my eyes to see Your work in my life. And
give me a grateful heart so I give You the glory for being
the hero of my story. In Jesus' name I pray. Amen.

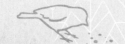

Why We Depend on God

*And don't think you can decide on your own what is right and what
is wrong. Respect the Eternal; turn and run from evil. If you depend
on Him, your body and mind will be free from the strain of a sinful life,
will experience healing and health, and will be strengthened at their core.*

PROVERBS 3:7–8 VOICE

Whether we recognize it or not, we need God's help. There's no doubt
about it. We need His help to live and love well because we don't have all
the answers. The problem is that many of us are used to going through
life on our own, making the decisions and choices we feel are best. We
get accustomed to being a solo act. We may have a few friends we go to
for advice, but for the most part we put our faith in ourselves to figure
things out.

Scripture tells us, however, that when we rely on God, our life and
relationships will be more harmonious. Including Him in our plans will
free us from the stress brought on by this sinful life. We'll be able to
make good decisions that glorify God and not our own flesh. And our
foundation of faith will be strengthened. The choice seems simple.

Father, I confess the times I've catered to my fleshly
desires rather than depending on You. Help me
place You at the core of my life so I can be blessed
by Your goodness. In Jesus' name I pray. Amen.

Faith Roots

But blessed is the man who trusts in the Lord and has made
the Lord his hope and confidence. He is like a tree planted along a
riverbank, with its roots reaching deep into the water—a tree not
bothered by the heat nor worried by long months of drought. Its leaves
stay green, and it goes right on producing all its luscious fruit.

JEREMIAH 17:7–8 TLB

Every time you choose to trust God with your circumstances, your faith roots deepen. When you surrender your fears and insecurities into His hands rather than try to fix things yourself, faith grips your heart more strongly. And as with a tree planted by water, the roots of your faith find nourishment unseen to the eye. It's an automatic response to thirst. It's sustenance always available and accessible. And this blessing is yours simply for choosing to plant yourself by the Source for all things.

Where do you draw hope from? How do you find peace? In this world—with things feeling so undone and unbalanced and ungodly—saturating yourself in the goodness of the Lord is more important than ever. Let Him nourish your weary soul. Let your faith be what sustains you. And cultivate a beautiful relationship with your Creator, making Him your hope and confidence.

Father, I want to be planted by You with roots that
sink deep into Your love. Be my nourishment and
sustenance in all things. In Jesus' name I pray. Amen.

Desperate Prayers

I'm desperate, Lord! I throw myself upon you, for you alone are my
God! My life, my every moment, my destiny—it's all in your hands.
So I know you can deliver me from those who persecute me relentlessly.

PSALM 31:14–15 TPT

Most of the time, we pray to God in a composed and controlled way. We have a list of what we need help with. We know who we want to pray for. We may use our prayer time to vent our frustrations, come clean about sins we've committed, or process life. And we may even let the Lord know the outcomes we're expecting. But other times when we go to God in prayer, we're begging for His hand to move mightily in our life. We're desperate. With every other option exhausted, we feel hopeless and panicked. And our prayer feels more like a plea for God to jump in and save us.

Let faith remind you it's safe to loosen your white-knuckle grip on the worrisome situations in your life and trust the Lord. He's your Deliverer. And it's okay to come to God worried and upset, because He knows exactly what you need in that moment. You can share the deepest places of pain with Him.

Father, I'm at the end of my rope. I've tried to fix it all
and have failed. I'm scared and overwhelmed. Grow my
faith in this moment to trust You're in control. Open my
eyes to see Your hand at work, and bring a peace that
calms my anxious heart. In Jesus' name I pray. Amen.

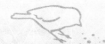

Who Is Your Champion?

Lord, you are my true strength and my glory-song, my champion, my Savior! The joyful songs I now sing will be sung again in the hearts and homes of all your devoted lovers. My loud shouts of victory will echo throughout the land. For Yahweh's right hand conquers valiantly!

PSALM 118:14–15 TPT

Think about who you would list as your true strength. Who do you consider a champion in your life? Many of us would point to some pretty amazing people God has put in our path. Maybe it's one of your parents who always comes through for you. It could be your husband who always seems to have right answers at every turn. It could be a teacher or coach who believed in you when no one else did. Or maybe it was a character from history whose life story gives you strength to be an overcomer.

If we're going to be women of faith, we have to place God at the top of the list. We need to discern all the ways He has made our lives better. Look for how the Lord has championed your work. See how He has strengthened you for the battles. Because God is the giver of all good things, let Him be the One who ultimately gets the credit.

Father, You're my true strength. You are my Champion. You're my Savior! All the glory goes to You for being so faithful in my life. In Jesus' name I pray. Amen.

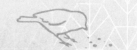

The Gratitude List

I will offer all my loving praise to you, and I thank you so much for answering my prayer and bringing me salvation!

PSALM 118:21 TPT

Just as we appreciate being recognized for a job well done or helping someone out, we ought to remember to heap our gratitude on God. Doing so is an important part of living a faith-filled life. Make it a point to thank Him for intervening in your life in meaningful ways. Let Him know you appreciate His help. Tell the Lord you recognize His hand moving in those tough situations. Talk to God about how His faithfulness changed the trajectory of your day. Praise Him for the gift of salvation.

What do you have to be thankful for right now? A restored relationship or rescue from a toxic one? The return of a prodigal child? Deliverance from an addiction? Financial relief? Job opportunities? Promising medical treatment? Today, take some time to create a gratitude list and then pray through it. Be lavish with your thanksgiving, giving God the glory He rightly deserves.

Father, You've helped me make sense of my messy life in so many ways. Today I've made a list and want to share it with You. This exercise filled my heart with gratitude as it revealed all the different areas where You've been faithful to me. Thank You! In Jesus' name I pray. Amen.

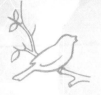

Fear of What Lies Ahead

Stay calm; there is no need to be afraid of a sudden disaster or to
worry when calamity strikes the wicked, for the Eternal is always
there to protect you. He will safeguard your each and every step.

PROVERBS 3:25–26 VOICE

Too often we live terrified of what's around the corner. We can't always see the danger ahead. Often there are no red flags or warning signs. We have no clues as to what's about to happen. But when we think of the future, all we see are horrible outcomes and dismal endings. We see destruction. We remember all the times we tried and failed. And we're pretty sure we'll face that same scenario again.

Let today's scripture passage be one you reference every time those negative thoughts pour into your heart. It's a powerful reminder to stay calm because God is with you. He's there to protect and keep you. And even when something horrible happens, the Lord will be with you through it all, guiding each step. The truth is, you *will* face hard seasons and situations, but your faith in God makes all the difference in the way you respond.

Father, give me courage to face what's ahead and trust You
through it. I don't expect a problem-free life, but remind me
that I can expect Your help as I navigate it. Keep me focused
on You, no matter what. In Jesus' name I pray. Amen.

The Prayer of Again

O God, please come and save us again;
bring us your breakthrough–victory!

PSALM 118:25 TPT

Again. We're so blessed to serve a God who doesn't grow tired of our repeat questions and pleas. He welcomes every request for a do-over or a re-up, and we're never made to feel guilty for asking. Think for a moment, friend. Just in the past week or so, how many times have you prayed for God to save you *again*? Or restore your marriage *again*. Refocus your child *again*. Restart your quiet time *again*. Reignite your passion *again*. Rebuild your business *again*.

Don't let anyone or anything keep you from going back to God. He will never grow weary of you or tired of the same requests. He knows we're often desperate for a breakthrough victory, and He specializes in them. When we're on our knees, desperate for God's help, we're able to see the manifestation of His love more clearly because we're on the lookout. And every answered "again" prayer builds our faith for the next time.

Father, what a relief to know I can ask over and over for the same thing and it isn't a problem in Your eyes. Thank You for not judging me or making me feel silly. It takes courage to ask for things on repeat. You know where my struggles are and understand why they're still with me. I'm asking You to help me again. In Jesus' name I pray. Amen.

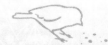

We Know God Can

For you are my high fortress, where I'm kept safe. You are to me
a stronghold of salvation. When you deliver me out of this peril,
it will bring glory to your name. As you guide me forth I'll be
kept safe from the hidden snares of the enemy—the secret traps
that lie before me—for you have become my rock of strength.

PSALM 31:3–4 TPT

The difference between having faith and not having faith is knowing God *can*. Unbelievers doubt Him on every level. They see Him as weak or uninterested. They don't understand His holiness and sovereignty. On the other hand, believers recognize God isn't bound by limitations. His power is full and complete, and so we don't waver on the question of *if*. We know we'll be delivered from the battle, but we're not sure how. We may not know His timing, but we know He'll show up. We can't predict His method, but we know God is in control.

So stand strong in your faith, friend. You don't need to have all the answers to trust God because you know He is your high fortress. He's your stronghold and strength. Because He is God, we can trust that He *can*. And our faith tells us He will.

Father, knowing You are a God who can—and will—
makes all the difference. Thank You for Your unmatched
faithfulness and unwavering love. In Jesus' name I pray. Amen.

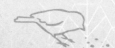

When We Get Bad News

They will not be afraid when the news is bad because they have resolved to trust in the Eternal. Their hearts are confident, and they are fearless, for they expect to see their enemies defeated.

PSALM 112:7–8 VOICE

No one likes to get bad news. We stick our fingers in our ears and sing la-la-la so we can't hear what's being spoken. We cover our eyes or turn away so we don't see the train wreck of a situation firsthand. And chances are we've become very good at finding ways to ignore the hard things in life. But we can't ignore them for long, right? Somehow they find their way onto center stage and we must deal with them whether we want to or not.

Let the psalmist's words be a reminder of the great God you serve. Choosing to put your trust in Him is a powerful act that removes the fear you're facing. It supernaturally breeds confidence and courage—so much so that your expectations are set on a win for you. God takes your fearful heart and makes it strong through your faith. Friend, bad news ain't got nothing on you.

Father, when bad news comes, remind me that I have nothing to fear because You are with me. Even more, You will fill me with confidence and an extra measure of faith. You are amazing! In Jesus' name I pray. Amen.

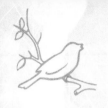

What to Do with a Troubled Heart

"Let not your heart be troubled.
You are trusting God, now trust in me."

John 14:1 TLB

What is troubling your heart today? Are you trying to process some bad news from a friend? Is your adult child struggling and your heart is breaking for their situation? Are your aging parents in deep decline and you're grieving the inevitable? Has life been unpredictable lately, and you dislike those kinds of surprises? Sometimes reading verses like today's frustrates us because our heart *is* troubled. We wonder what we're doing wrong. We wonder why our life can't be more carefree. We feel like failures. But maybe the reason is found in the next sentence.

If we don't let our faith rise up so we can trust God with our suffering, it will wear us down. We will absolutely feel the effects of the challenges we face if we don't engage the Lord's help. We must lean on Him as we walk the dusty path. The truth is that God must be the One to lead us through the valley if we have a hope of getting to the other side intact.

Father, You know every reason my heart is heavy. You see every situation that breaks me. You catch every tear that falls. Meet me in the middle of my brokenness and bring peace and restoration. Teach me to anchor my faith in You. In Jesus' name I pray. Amen.

Jesus Is the Only Way

*Jesus told him, "I am the Way—yes, and the Truth and the Life.
No one can get to the Father except by means of me. If you had
known who I am, then you would have known who my Father
is. From now on you know him—and have seen him!"*

JOHN 14:6–7 TLB

Jesus is the Way, the Truth, and the Life. When you anchor your faith in Him—believing He is God's Son who died on the cross for your sins—you are saved. And scripture tells us there is *no other way* we can get to heaven but through that faith. Let it sink in.

Friend, so many untruths are lurking out there, telling you their way of thinking is correct. They promise salvation through all the wrong avenues, and many get sucked into the lies. That's why knowing the truth is so important. Don't let the world sway you or bring doubt. And remember, you can always refer to the Bible to know what is real and right. It is God's holy Word and the authority on all things. Have faith!

**Father, thank You for Your Son, Jesus. Thank You for who
He is to me and what He did to save me. Help me stand
solid and strong in my belief that His death on the
cross secured my eternity with You in heaven. I know
He is the only way. In Jesus' name I pray. Amen.**

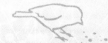

When Grief Lasts

O Lord, help me again! Keep showing me such mercy. For I am in
anguish, always in tears, and I'm worn out with weeping. I'm becoming
old because of grief; my health is broken. I'm exhausted! My life is spent
with sorrow, my years with sighing and sadness. Because of all these
troubles, I have no more strength. My inner being is so weak and frail.

PSALM 31:9–10 TPT

We all face those moments when we're overwhelmed by sorrow. Sadness is one of the toughest seasons to navigate because we feel it so deeply. Life is a series of losses, and each one hurts at a cellular level. We face grief when someone we love dies. We feel distress when our relationships are struggling. We live with regret over missed opportunities. And we are burdened when we get tangled up in the details of someone else's mess.

When you hit those times of weakness and woe, let the experience be a red flag that you're taking on too much alone. God will help you carry the sorrow as you process through it. He will help you release it when appropriate. And in His kindness, God will bring you joy once again as you lean into Him.

Father, how can I function when I'm in a constant state of
sorrow? How can I live in victory when all I feel is defeat?
Please help me again. In Jesus' name I pray. Amen.

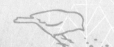

Be a Light in the Dark

When life is dark, a light will shine for those who live rightly—
those who are merciful, compassionate, and strive for justice.

<small>Psalm 112:4 VOICE</small>

Let's be honest: the world is filled with much darkness today. Society continues to take a nosedive morally and seems determined to drag those we love with it. What is inappropriate and wrong, the world now says is right. And what is decent and right, the world now shouts is wrong. Walking out our faith is getting harder and harder in a world hostile to it. Now more than ever, we need God's help.

When you let your faith rise up, you'll see His light shining through the darkness. The Lord is looking for the faithful who are filled with mercy and compassion and working toward justice to stand strong and combat the forces of darkness. With His strength and your resolve, you can shine a light for the Lord for all to see.

Father, it's easy to give in to frustration and hopelessness when I see how messed up this world is. How did we get here so quickly? Things feel dark and hopeless, but I know that when I keep my faith ignited by Your goodness, it will be a guide for me. Help my life to be a light for others—one that shines Your hope into the world. In Jesus' name I pray. Amen.

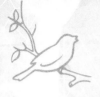

The God of Breakthroughs

So cheer up! Take courage, all you who love him. Wait for
him to break through for you, all who trust in him!

PSALM 31:24 TPT

Do you ever give in to the doom-and-gloom feelings and walk around defeated? Do you mope all day long, hoping someone notices? At times we all wear our emotions on our sleeve because we want sympathy. We may be able to tuck away our stress and strife most of the time, but sometimes we want others to see our pain. It may be a passive-aggressive way to get what we really want—attention.

But we have access to hope and peace because of our faith in God. He will lift us out of the mire and shower us with His love. It takes courage to ask for help, especially when life feels dark and overwhelming. Many times we want to crawl into bed and pull the covers over our head. We hide from community and suffer alone. But we serve a God of breakthroughs, and when we place our faith in Him, we can be assured a breakthrough is coming.

Father, I'm weary today and can't seem to catch a break.
I confess I've tried to garner support by moping. I've even
hidden out from those who care about me. But now I'm
activating my faith instead, trusting You'll bring the breakthrough I need at the right time. In Jesus' name I pray. Amen.

Transformed from the Inside Out

Stop imitating the ideals and opinions of the culture around you,
but be inwardly transformed by the Holy Spirit through a total
reformation of how you think. This will empower you to discern God's
will as you live a beautiful life, satisfying and perfect in his eyes.

ROMANS 12:2 TPT

When you commit to God, He will transform you from the inside out. He will change your heart and rewire your desires. His Holy Spirit in you will prompt those gut feelings designed to lead you on the paths of righteousness. Your mind will crave to know more about God as you pursue Him every day. And you will feel empowered to live and love in ways that glorify the Lord. These are all byproducts of faith.

So be intentional about refusing to let the world speak into your life. Just stop giving it a position of power. Don't allow it to influence how you think or what you pay attention to. Pursue the things of God so the inward transformation can happen. It's the best way to live.

Father, change me. Bring healing and restoration. Transform me so my heart is for You and not for the things of the world. Let me crave You above all else. And help me focus on following Your will and ways. I'm grateful Your heart is always for me. In Jesus' name I pray. Amen.

Designed to Work Together

In the human body there are many parts and organs, each with a unique function. And so it is in the body of Christ. For though we are many, we've all been mingled into one body in Christ. This means that we are all vitally joined to one another, with each contributing to the others.

ROMANS 12:4–5 TPT

We're to work as a team—at least that's the plan. When God created each of us, He did so with the express purpose of being joined with one another. You have something special to share with the body of Christ, and they have something amazing to share with you too—teamwork! We can support one another as we share the Good News with the world. The Lord knits all of us together so every angle is covered. What an amazing design!

That's why God values relationships. It's why He puts certain people in your path. It's why He puts missions and service on your heart. Community is a great way to walk out your faith with other like-minded believers. And the Lord will use it to grow not only you but those around you as well.

> Father, You really do think of everything. You made us to be like pieces of a puzzle, working together in community with a common purpose. I'm grateful for the skills I've been given! Use me to further the kingdom and point others to You in heaven! In Jesus' name I pray. Amen.

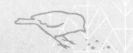

Good Things Stored Up

Lord, how wonderful you are! You have stored up so many good things for us, like a treasure chest heaped up and spilling over with blessings—all for those who honor and worship you! Everybody knows what you can do for those who turn and hide themselves in you.

PSALM 31:19 TPT

What a powerful and fun visual. To think God has stored up good things for us is exciting. It's like when you start buying birthday or Christmas presents for those you love, and you begin tucking them away for the big reveal. You may shop for months leading up to the event, stockpiling items you know will delight your friend or family member. And at the right moment, you bring them out and bless them.

Scripture says God does the same thing for us. In His kindness and generosity, the Lord is storing up goodness for those who honor and worship Him. Your faith places you in that group! And you can only imagine how much more amazing His heavenly gifts are compared to the ones we can purchase here. So be a woman of faith, loving the Lord with all your heart, mind, soul, and strength. And be blessed!

Father, thinking of all You've stored up for me almost makes me giddy. It puts a huge smile on my face and makes me feel loved, especially because I don't get many gifts these days. You're the best. In Jesus' name I pray. Amen.

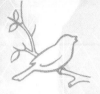

Just Be Real

Let the inner movement of your heart always be to love one another,
and never play the role of an actor wearing a mask. Despise evil
and embrace everything that is good and virtuous. Be devoted to
tenderly loving your fellow believers as members of one family.
Try to outdo yourselves in respect and honor of one another.

ROMANS 12:9–10 TPT

Nothing is more frustrating than discovering inauthenticity in someone. When we discover they're not who they've pretended to be, we're thrown off balance. It could be the revelation of a husband's secret life or the sinking realization that a friend has shared your secrets with others. Maybe a coworker takes your idea and presents it as their own, or perhaps a child who you thought was following the rules is unexpectedly caught in a series of lies. Trusting that someone is being honest is part of loving them, which is why it hurts so bad when the truth comes out.

Be the kind of woman who lives with transparency. Just be yourself—stumbles, fumbles, and all. The goal isn't to be perfect. It's to be real, accepting that mistakes are part of life and being open about them. There's no reason to wear a mask to hide the truth. Your brokenness is beautiful.

Father, give me the courage to be honest about
my life. I want to live with authenticity in
every way. In Jesus' name I pray. Amen.

The Challenge to Speak Blessings

Speak blessing, not cursing, over those
who reject and persecute you.

Romans 12:14 TPT

This may be one of the hardest commands to keep. Who wants to speak blessings when someone is hating on them? Who wants to speak words of life when others are talking smack about them or someone they love? Returning blessing for cursing is not easy to do on any level, which is why we must trust the Lord to change our heart.

If you ask Him, God will allow you to see your oppressors the way He does. You will be able to see their brokenness. You will see the effects of the difficult road they've had to walk. You may see their battle with jealousy or envy. Maybe they are lashing out at you from an overflow of rage they hold towards others. These reasons don't make their mistreatment of you okay—not at all. Nothing justifies their behavior. But if you will rise up in faith, God will give you a unique perspective into what lies behind their actions. And maybe you'll be willing and able to use kind words instead of saying what might make you feel better in the moment.

Father, open my eyes to see what's behind the hate. And
give me the ability to speak with love rather than out
of my own response of hurt. I need Your help to speak
blessings, not curses. In Jesus' name I pray. Amen.

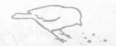

When You Feel like Nobody

*My enemies say, "You are nothing!" Even my friends and
neighbors hold me in contempt! They dread seeing me, and they look
the other way when I pass by. I am totally forgotten, buried away
like a dead man, discarded like a broken dish thrown in the trash.*

PSALM 31:11–12 TPT

So often I feel like a nobody. I feel unseen and unloved. People tell me I'm
either too much or too little, and their comments leave me questioning
my value. There are those who hate me for reasons I don't understand.
They criticize me, making me feel small and insignificant. I'm ridiculed
for the words I say, the emotions I feel, and the things I do. And while
I try to live and love well with a heart full of generosity for others, I feel
myself shutting down.

My faith tells me I'm fearfully and wonderfully made. I know I'm an
intentional creation, made on purpose and for a purpose. Please reignite
that truth in me today, Lord. Remind me I am loved by You. Tell me
again what makes me special. And bring people into my life to encourage and stand with me. Bring me peace and joy once again.

Father, You're the One I need to hear from today. Your voice is
what I need to hear deep in my spirit, reaffirming my value. I'm
overwhelmed by mean-spiritedness and desperate for Your
kindness and gentleness right now. In Jesus' name I pray. Amen.

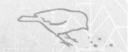

Let God Be Your Source

*The Eternal is the source of my strength and the shield
that guards me. When I learn to rest and truly trust Him,
He sends His help. This is why my heart is singing! I open
my mouth to praise Him, and thankfulness rises as song.*

PSALM 28:7 VOICE

When you grab onto the truth that God is your Source for all things, it will change your perspective on life. Your stress level will decrease because you know He will provide. Your fear will dissipate because you believe He is mighty to save. Your insecurities will diminish as you realize your value and identity rest in Him. You'll have confidence because you'll realize you're backed by the Creator. You will find peace because you don't have to be in control. And you can have a sense of joy knowing everything will work out according to His will, which is always in your favor.

Take a moment to thank God for being your Source. Let your voice praise Him for the unwavering love He offers. Tell the Lord what He means to you. Your faithfulness to trust Him in all things and to recognize His sovereignty delights His heart.

Father, there is no doubt that You are my Source. I see the
ways You have blessed me and kept me, and I am so thankful
for the fierce love You show. In Jesus' name I pray. Amen.

The Power of the Word

Let the words from the book of the law be always on your lips.
Meditate on them day and night so that you may be careful to
live by all that is written in it. If you do, as you make your way
through this world, you will prosper and always find success.

Joshua 1:8 voice

If you don't spend time in God's Word, how will you be able to walk out today's verse? God reveals Himself through the pages of the Bible, giving us insight into the way He works. We read the stories of those who walked with Jesus and spent time in God's presence. We find encouragement from the stories of people who were saved and delivered, healed and restored. And the Lord links knowing the Word to prospering and finding success.

Your faith will rise up and grow when you invest in the Bible. How are you doing with that? Why not carve out time each day to read a verse or two or even a chapter or two and think on them. Ask God what He wants to say to you. Ask Him what nugget of truth you should take away. And ask for deeper insight into how it relates to your life today.

Father, thank You for Your Word! What a gift to leave Your
children. Cultivate in me a love and a desire to know You
better through the Holy Bible. In Jesus' name I pray. Amen.

Nothing in This World Will Save

See those people polishing their chariots, and those others grooming their horses? But we're making garlands for GOD our God. The chariots will rust, those horses pull up lame—and we'll be on our feet, standing tall.

PSALM 20:7–8 MSG

Nothing in this world will save you. Yes, some things can improve your quality of life, like medicine, a healthy lifestyle, honest living, and trusted friends. But to place your faith in the here and now will always leave you wanting more. In the end, you'll come up short every time. Because what's here is temporal and what God offers through faith is eternal.

We aren't to despise the world, but neither are we to fully embrace what it offers. Jesus is our Savior, amen? And keep in mind that little eyes are watching you, so set the right example for them to follow. Model to those around you that God is our hope. Show them He is the source of peace. Let them know where to anchor their faith.

> Father, help me remember that nothing in this
> world can truly save me. Help me establish healthy
> boundaries so I don't get caught up in earthly promises.
> You are my Savior and the One who can meet every need.
> It's all about You, Lord. In Jesus' name I pray. Amen.

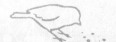

Meet Their Loathing with Love

If your enemy is hungry, buy him lunch! Win him over
with kindness. For your surprising generosity will awaken
his conscience, and God will reward you with favor.

ROMANS 12:20 TPT

How can we be kind to our enemies when we're busy bad-mouthing them? How can we bless them when all we do is bash them? We can't be generous while we're being hateful at the same time. It's one or the other. Either we love them or we hate them.

Who would you consider your enemies? A former spouse? Your boss? The nosy neighbor? A former friend? God is asking you to be kind to them. He wants you to bless them if the opportunity arises. The Lord wants you to meet their loathing with love. Return their cattiness with compassion. And when you activate your faith in this way, God will reward you with favor.

Father, I'm going to need Your help to walk this out. I confess my pride gets in the way and the last thing I want to do is be nice to those who don't like me. I can be wretched in my own flesh. Please change my heart so I can see my enemies from Your perspective and treat them with the kindness and generosity You expect. In Jesus' name I pray. Amen.

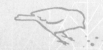

Everything Is Going to Work Out

*That clinches it—help's coming, an answer's
on the way, everything's going to work out.*

PSALM 20:6 MSG

Everything is going to work out! You can take that to the bank. And everything will end in a way that benefits you and brings glory to God. This is true no matter what. Believe it. Have faith and stand strong. But, friend, also be brave. Why? Because things may not end the way you asked or the way you imagined. Here is where your faith comes into play.

You have the freedom to ask the Lord for what you need, so what is it? Do you need a marriage restored? A lie exposed? The root of a fear revealed? Do you crave peace or joy? Are you searching for wisdom or discernment? Is a hard conversation around the corner? Tell God your needs and then have faith that an answer is on the way. And even if things end up differently than you imagined, know that everything is going to work out according to His beautiful plan.

Father, grow my faith so that I can rest in the truth
that You are in control. Let me find peace in the process,
knowing all will work out. You are sovereign and full of
compassion, and I believe You will meet my needs in the best
way possible and at the perfect time. In Jesus' name I pray. Amen.

Listening for God's Voice

*Eternal One, I am calling out to You; You are the foundation of my
life. Please, don't turn Your ear from me. If You respond to my pleas
with silence, I will lose all hope like those silenced by death's grave.*

PSALM 28:1 VOICE

Sometimes what we need more than anything else is to hear the voice of
God. It's not usually an audible voice, but He speaks to us nonetheless.
How do you hear Him?

God often speaks through His Word—the Bible. You may read a
passage that jumps out at you. Maybe you've read it a million times, but
this time it feels fresh. God speaks through worship music, like when the
chorus brings you to tears. He speaks through nature, especially during
those times of awe when we realize the magnitude of the Lord. It may
even be a consistent and persistent message we receive often and over
a short period of time. Or it could be an overwhelming feeling we get
during prayer when something presses on our heart. Regardless, any word
from God is a faith-builder.

**Father, give me spiritual ears to hear Your beautiful
and powerful voice in my life. Let me be listening for You
throughout the day, always aware of Your presence. You are
the foundation of my life, and I long to hear what You have to
say. My faith is secure in You. In Jesus' name I pray. Amen.**

Believe and Proclaim

For if you tell others with your own mouth that Jesus
Christ is your Lord and believe in your own heart that
God has raised him from the dead, you will be saved.

ROMANS 10:9 TLB

Believe and proclaim. It's so important you understand who Jesus is and what He did on the cross. You need to know He was raised from the dead three days later by the Father and how that affects you in the here and now. But equally as important as believing, you must speak of your faith to others. You must tell them about Jesus so they can believe too. Help them understand what He did for them. Talk to them about why it matters that they have faith as well.

You have the unique opportunity to lead others to the foot of the cross. You don't need to stand on the street corner with signs or a loudspeaker. You don't need to have all the answers. Instead, share your story of how Jesus intervened in your life. Be open about why your faith is secure in Him. And be sure they know how they can accept Jesus as their personal Savior too.

Father, I've always felt intimidated about leading others
to faith because I've considered myself ill-equipped.
But my job is simply to share the experiences I've had
with You. I'm to tell others about who You are to me.
The rest is up to You. In Jesus' name I pray. Amen.

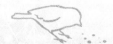

When We Want to Plot Revenge

Never hold a grudge or try to get even, but plan your life around the noblest way to benefit others. Do your best to live as everybody's friend.
ROMANS 12:17–18 TPT

Oh, it can feel so good in the moment to plot revenge. We think of countless ways we can get back at someone who has hurt us. We think about how to embarrass them or expose the kind of person they are. We ponder how to ruin their reputation. We daydream of what we would say given the chance to tell them off. And we often involve others, trying to garner sympathy and recruit them to be on our team. Chances are we never follow through on our plots, but giving potential revenge space in our thought life is a waste of time.

Instead, God wants us to plan our life around things noble and decent. He wants us to live and love in ways that benefit those around us. We're to be friendly and kind whenever possible. And honestly, God has to be the One to make this possible, especially when our hurt feelings take over. Let your faith rise up so you can respond to offenses with a pure heart focused on living God's way. He will make it possible!

Father, change my heart so I'm able to see those who hurt me through Your eyes. Help me choose to respond in love rather than plot revenge. In Jesus' name I pray. Amen.

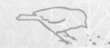

The Peace That Comes from God

"I'm leaving you well and whole. That's my parting gift to you.
Peace. I don't leave you the way you're used to being left—
feeling abandoned, bereft. So don't be upset. Don't be distraught."

JOHN 14:27 MSG

Because of our faith, we have access to the Lord's peace, which is unmatched by anything the world offers. Even more, it's often an immediate gift when we cry out for it. It floods our heart and brings a palpable calm. And there's a measure of much-needed hope mixed in, so we don't end up in a pit of discouragement and depression. So why do we spend so much time trying to find peace apart from God?

Where do you need His peace today? Where are you struggling with anxiety? What worries keep you up at night? From relationship issues to financial woes to fear of the future, we are bombarded with real-life situations that stir up our emotions. Be quick to take each one to God and ask Him to exchange it for His peace that surpasses all understanding. Trust Him to bring calm to your fearful heart. And remember that God's plans for you are filled with hope. With Him, you can live in the freedom peace brings!

Father, I don't want the kind of peace the world offers.
It's counterfeit. Fill me with Your peace and let it reign
in my anxious heart! In Jesus' name I pray. Amen.

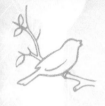

The Trap of Fear and Intimidation

Fear and intimidation is a trap that holds you back. But when you place your confidence in the Lord, you will be seated in the high place.

PROVERBS 29:25 TPT

Don't cower or turn away. Stand tall and hold your own. Don't allow circumstances to intimidate you into silence. Say what needs to be said. Push away the fear that tries to trap you in a death spiral. You serve a God who is mighty to save. Remember, you are a daughter of the Most High, and God is very protective of His children.

So how do you walk out this kind of confidence? By letting your faith rise up. When you choose to believe you are who God says you are, and when you realize He is in control of this crazy world, you will find the confidence to stand tall. You won't care as much what people think about you. You won't battle those feelings of insecurity on such epic levels. You won't search for earthly significance because you'll understand your value is anchored in the Lord. And, friend, that makes you royalty.

Father, I will place my confidence in You. I will choose to believe I am significant and loved. I will remember You created me on purpose and for a purpose. And I will be intentional to cling to You when I feel weak and fearful, because I know You will strengthen me again and again. In Jesus' name I pray. Amen.

When You're Called to Lead

We will do all you have commanded, and we will go wherever you send us. We will follow your orders just as we obeyed Moses in all he told us. May the Eternal One, your God, be with you as He was with Moses.

JOSHUA 1:16–17 VOICE

The Israelite leaders were vowing to follow Joshua as the new commander in chief after Moses died. God called up Joshua to take command and filled him with the courage to take charge. Just as the Lord did for this new leader, He will do for you too. Joshua had no choice but to trust God as he stepped into this new role. The job required leading the Israelites into the Promised Land. So he had to believe—had to have the faith—that God would reveal every next step.

Do you feel God is calling you into leadership? What an honor and privilege to be used by God in such an awesome way. Be it leading your family, a ministry, a company, a Bible study, or any other opportunity, you are responsible for being steeped in the Word so you can clearly hear God. Take it seriously. And let your faith guide you as others follow.

Father, I'm terrified to step into leadership because I feel unworthy. Give me the courage and confidence to follow You, knowing You'll lead the way. In Jesus' name I pray. Amen.

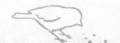

The Spirit of Harmony

Live happily together in a spirit of harmony, and be as mindful
of another's worth as you are your own. Don't live with a lofty
mind-set, thinking you are too important to serve others, but be
willing to do menial tasks and identify with those who are humble
minded. Don't be smug or even think for a moment that you know it all.

ROMANS 12:16 TPT

Sometimes we feel like we're all that and a bag of chips. We think we're the cat's meow. For a variety of reasons, we end up with an inflated vision of who we are. It's not like we're supposed to hate ourselves or feel inferior, but God isn't impressed by our self-righteous attitude. As a matter of fact, He actually tells us to reject it.

When we put ourselves above others, we will naturally look down on them. But when instead we focus on creating harmony, we level the playing field and allow ourselves to see the needs of others. God, through our faith, makes harmony with others possible, and it's a beautiful image of the kind of community He created for us. Working together, serving together, and caring for one another in meaningful ways are all harmony-building actions that delight the Lord.

Father, keep my pride in check so it doesn't get me
in trouble. I want to live in harmony with others,
and I can't do that if I feel loftier than them. Knit
my heart to theirs. In Jesus' name I pray. Amen.

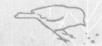

The World's Riches
Are Short-Lived

Don't follow after the wicked ones or be jealous of their
wealth. Don't think for a moment they're better off than you.
They and their short-lived success will soon shrivel up and
quickly fade away, like grass clippings in the hot sun.

PSALM 37:1–2 TPT

Whatever riches the world has to offer are short lived. The reality is that you can't take them with you, amen? You can't stuff your pockets with money as you walk into heaven. You can't bring the massive flat-screen TV or the diamond earrings. The tricked-out truck stays as well as the countless shoes and purses you've collected over the years. None of it comes with you.

So what if rather than working hard to collect stuff to keep up with those around you, you instead focused on growing your faith? It's easy to be jealous of what others have, but it keeps your eyes off God. You may think others have more or are more, but remember that your immeasurable value is anchored in heaven. And every time you choose the Lord over the world's treasures, He sees and honors your choice.

Father, nothing the world has to offer is better than You. A life of faith is unmatched by earthly riches. Let me remember this truth when I feel the tug of keeping up. Let me cry to You when I feel less than others. You are all I need. In Jesus' name I pray. Amen.

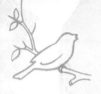

100 Percent Faithful

If you're faithful in small-scale matters, you'll be
faithful with far bigger responsibilities. If you're crooked
in small responsibilities, you'll be no different in bigger things.

LUKE 16:10 VOICE

Let your faith rise up whether you're facing a small issue or a massive one. Treat them the same way, making good choices that reflect your belief in God. Invite Him into every moment, little or large. Be the same person whether you're facing minor challenges or major ones. The reality is, the way you respond to the small is a good indicator of the way you'll respond to the big. So be full of faith no matter what.

Why do you think your attitude matters to God? Why do you think He cares? A consistent approach to life's challenges reveals the authenticity of your heart for righteousness. Are you willing to walk out your faith when the stakes are low, or do you only trust God with the big stuff? Is He always on your mind or just in situations that feel overwhelming? Do your actions reflect your faith in every situation or just in the ones with a bigger audience? Choose to be the kind of woman who is faithful 100 percent of the time.

Father, I'm all in. I don't want to have a fair-weather
faith. Help my faith rise up in both the big and the
small things. In Jesus' name I pray. Amen.

The Choice of Right and Wrong

Keep trusting in the Lord and do what is right in his eyes. Fix your heart on the promises of God, and you will dwell in the land, feasting on his faithfulness.

PSALM 37:3 TPT

When you're faced with the choice to do right or wrong, choose to do right. That may sound simple and silly to say, but so often we deliberately decide to do wrong. We think we'll do what we want and apologize to God later. We do serve a God of second chances, right? And without hesitation, we too often give in to the flesh and turn our back on God.

Instead, let's focus on the Lord's promises to help us choose right. When we're in a bind, He will save. When we're in a mess, He will deliver. When we need strength to say no, God will give it. When we need hope or peace, it's ours for the asking. So in those moments when you're walking the thin line between right and wrong, trust the Lord to keep His word. He is faithful in everything and always will be.

Father, I confess the times I've made bad choices because I knew I would be forgiven. I'm sorry for not exercising my faith to stand strong. Make my faith rise up so I can keep my eyes fixed on You and Your promises. In Jesus' name I pray. Amen.

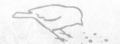

The Love of Money

You've made your choice. Your ambition is to look good in front of other people, not God. But God sees through to your hearts. He values things differently from you. The goals you and your peers are reaching for God detests.

LUKE 16:15 VOICE

In today's verse, Jesus is talking to the Pharisees about their love of money. He is making the point that it's impossible to serve two gods—both the one true God and money. One will naturally be more important than the other, and a choice will need to be made. Jesus knew the Pharisees loved money above the Lord God. If you think about it, do you too?

Remember that money is not the problem. The *love* of money is the problem. When you use riches to elevate yourself above others, the love of money shows itself to be an issue. When you worship earthly treasures over God, your life becomes unhealthy. When money—making it or spending it—is what you focus on the most with your time and effort, you may need to reevaluate. Friend, the Lord's values should be what you strive for. What He finds important is what you should find important as well. And your faith should drive your heart toward Him more than anything the world can offer.

Father, investigate my heart and reveal to me when I am loving anything over You. Help me recognize when my goals are not in alignment with Yours. I want to value the same things You do so I can glorify You with my life. In Jesus' name I pray. Amen.

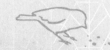

God Will Make Up the Difference

It is much better to have little combined with much of God than
to have the fabulous wealth of the wicked and nothing else.

PSALM 37:16 TPT

Let God be the One to make up the difference. Let Him be the One to fill the gaps in your life. Scripture tells us it's better to have little and depend on God to be big than the other way around.

Do you need a big miracle in your marriage? Are you losing hope for getting pregnant or hearing positive news from the adoption agency? Are you down to the last bit of money in savings and desperate for a job? Is your small business struggling to makes ends meet and you're not sure where else to turn? Have you lost someone close to you and now you feel lost? Ask God to add to your little. His economy is unmatched. In His great love, He will multiply your portion until your needs are met. Never forget that the Lord sees you. And your faith lets God know you see Him too.

Father, You know where I'm lacking and need help. You see every need I have even before I do. I'm trusting You to fill in the gaps so I can live in plenty. It's not that I need abundance. It's that I need enough. I believe in You, and I know Your heart for me is always good. In Jesus' name I pray. Amen.

Why We Cling to God

"Because he clings to Me in love, I will rescue him from harm;
I will set him above danger. Because he has known Me by
name, He will call on Me, and I will answer. I'll be with him
through hard times; I'll rescue him and grant him honor."

PSALM 91:14–15 VOICE

With God on your side, you're victorious. That doesn't mean you won't go through very tough seasons in life. It won't keep you from heartbreaking moments or ensure a trouble-free existence. You will most certainly struggle in relationships. Finances will be cause for concern at times. You will lose those you care about the most. And your body will suffer from the aging process no matter how hard you fight back. It's all part of the human condition, living in a fallen world.

But hope comes from our faith that God sees us, loves us, and is intimately involved in our lives. When we cling to Him through the difficulties, we can be assured a rescue. When we're at the end of us and desperate to find a way out, He will be like a guiding light. God will illuminate the path forward as He walks it with us. Don't be discouraged. Instead, be encouraged knowing the Lord will always answer.

Father, rescue me from the hardships
I'm facing. Help me trust You to navigate me
through to freedom. In Jesus' name I pray. Amen.

Always Seen by God

*Day by day the Lord watches the good deeds of the godly,
and he prepares for them his forever-reward. Even in a time
of disaster he will watch over them, and they will always
have more than enough no matter what happens.*

PSALM 37:18–19 TPT

God sees all the good you do that goes unnoticed by others. He sees how early you get up to prepare breakfast for your family. He sees the gift bag left anonymously on your neighbor's porch. He sees the twenty-dollar bill you hand the homeless man on the side of the road. God sees the effort you put into making the holidays special in your home. He sees the hours you spend on your knees in prayer, fighting for those you love. He sees it all.

Sometimes we get frustrated thinking we're unseen—and maybe we are. There's a good chance most of the helpful and virtuous things you do go unnoticed. But never by God. So often others receive the benefit of your good deeds without understanding the thought, time, and effort that went into them. In those moments, let God remind you that your faith in Him is beautiful, and so is your servant's heart for those around you.

**Father, thank You for knowing my heart's desire to
be seen. And thank You for always noticing what I
do to bless others. In Jesus' name I pray. Amen.**

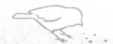

Go to God First

*The Lord is good. When trouble comes, he is the place
to go! And he knows everyone who trusts in him!*

NAHUM 1:7 TLB

Where do you go when trouble comes? The world offers no shortage of options. It's always ready to provide a quick solution with big promises and short-lived results. In those moments, we want to numb ourselves from feeling the pain. We're looking to stop the hemorrhaging fast. And so often we reach for the world's options first. They are the low-hanging fruit. But in the end, we feel cheated because the results didn't satisfy our deepest needs. We're left with buyer's remorse.

What if you went to God first? When the difficult phone call comes, let Him be your first stop. When you get the bad news, drop to your knees and pray. Why not reach out to the One who can immediately and effectively calm the raging storm in your spirit? It takes grit in those moments to let your faith rise up, but when you go to the Source of comfort with your broken heart, it will be beautifully restored.

Father, I confess I've looked to earthly solutions for my pain
and hurt. And even though those solutions never satisfy,
I keep going back. Break that cycle in me so I go to You first.
I know You're the only One who can meet my needs and
mend the broken places in me. In Jesus' name I pray. Amen.

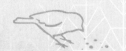

Beautiful Benefits

But the Lord will be the Savior of all who love him. Even in their
time of trouble, God will live in them as strength. Because of their
faith in him, their daily portion will be a Father's help and deliverance
from evil. This is true for all who turn to hide themselves in him!

PSALM 37:39–40 TPT

In the verses above, did you catch the part that said for those who love the Lord, God "will live in them as strength"? When your faith is anchored in Him, you will receive His help and deliverance every day. Friend, there are beautiful benefits to believing in the Lord and trusting Him with your heart.

But make sure you don't love God for manipulative reasons. We aren't playing house with our faith, pretending to care about living a righteous life because of what we get out of it. Instead, we choose to surrender to the One we trust above all else. We invest in the relationship. We go to Him to meet our needs. We wait on Him with expectation. And when we do, He will be our daily portion!

Father, You're the One I love and trust with my life. You're
the One who will meet my needs and care for my heart.
Hide me in You and help me live in ways that glorify
Your holy name. And thank You for the beautiful benefits
that come with faith. In Jesus' name I pray. Amen.

Using Your Words for Good

Nothing is more appealing than speaking beautiful, life-giving words.
For they release sweetness to our souls and inner healing to our spirits.

PROVERBS 16:24 TPT

Let your words be full of encouragement. There are enough rude and mean-spirited comments flying around. We hear hurtful remarks on the regular. People make unkind statements without thinking and we're left devastated. And we've all been subjected to people sharing their thoughts under the guise of being "helpful." What we need are kind people saying kind things.

Even if you must have a difficult conversation, you can still choose your words wisely. Ask God to guide you to speak the truth in life-giving ways, and He will. With His help, you can discipline without dismantling. Carefully determining the things you will say can bring healing to a weary spirit. Speaking uplifting words can bring sweetness to the soul. And being faithful to listen for God's direction can make all the difference in the world when you interact with others.

> Father, I've been the victim of mean words, so I appreciate the heart behind this verse. Thank You for including things like this in Your Word. I don't want to be reckless with what I say. Give me a sensitivity to Your Holy Spirit so I can follow His leading in tense situations. Let me be kind and generous always. In Jesus' name I pray. Amen.

Cry Out to God

So don't be afraid. I am here, with you; don't be dismayed,
for I am your God. I will strengthen you, help you. I am here
with My right hand to make right and to hold you up.

ISAIAH 41:10 VOICE

Yes, things are tough right now. You're facing battles on every front and it makes sense you are tired. Of course you're feeling weary and losing hope. Nothing is easy in this season. Chances are you've considered giving up or walking away. You've been doing the very best you can with what you have to work with.

How is your relationship with God right now? Have you invited Him into your mess? Today's verse outlines why your faith is so important. When you activate your faith, God promises to be with you to fend off fear and dismay. He promises to give you strength through the process. He will provide the help you need when you need it and will hold you up through every difficult season. Friend, don't wait a moment longer to cry out.

Father, I'm overwhelmed by my life right now. And while I've tried to handle things on my own, I can't do it any longer. I need You to intervene as only You can. I need hope that things can change. I need relief from the barrage of challenges. And I need Your strength to hold me up as we walk out this season together. Please help me. In Jesus' name I pray. Amen.

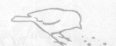

In All Circumstances

Have faith in Him in all circumstances, dear people. Open up
your heart to Him; the True God shelters us in His arms.
PSALM 62:8 VOICE

Like most, you probably trust God deeply in some areas of your life. You believe what He says is true, and so you don't struggle to let go and let God. But then there are areas where you can't seem to release control. For so long you've been the one in the driver's seat. You've searched for answers and made ends meet. And the idea of letting go of the wheel feels way too scary.

The truth is that God wants you to have faith in Him in all circumstances—relationships, finances, health, parenting, insecurities, career. Why? Because He has a vested interest in every part of your life. No detail is too small or issue too big. And God knows you'll find relief and security in His arms. In Him you can have a sense of safety unmatched by anything or anyone else. Let your faith rise up as you run to the Lord for shelter. Let Him be with you through it all.

Father, forgive me for keeping You at arm's length. Some of my struggles have been harder to turn over than others, and my grip on them is tight. Give me the confidence to release everything to You as my faith in Your sovereignty matures. Help me trust You with everything. In Jesus' name I pray. Amen.

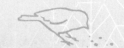

When You Need
God to Show Up

Come quickly, Lord, and answer me, for my depression deepens; don't turn away from me or I shall die. Let me see your kindness to me in the morning, for I am trusting you. Show me where to walk, for my prayer is sincere. Save me from my enemies. O Lord, I run to you to hide me.

Psalm 143:7–9 TLB

The psalmist is asking God for full coverage. From the depths of depression, he is begging for the Lord to overtake his life and cover every angle. Have you ever felt that level of angst before? The kind where you know how deeply you need God to show up?

The writer is pleading for answers. He is asking God to stay focused on the situation. He is insisting on seeing God's kindness first thing in the morning, right as his eyes open. He wants the Lord to guide every step of the day and save him from enemies. And he wants the Lord to tuck him away for safekeeping. Can you relate? Friend, God will do all these things for you and more. Have faith and ask.

Father, I understand the desperation of the psalmist. I know what he must have been feeling because I'm feeling it too. Hear the cry of my heart and come quickly. You're my only hope and I'm clinging to You with all my strength. In Jesus' name I pray. Amen.

See God as Number One

"Cursed is the strong one who depends on mere humans, who thinks
he can make it on muscle alone and sets GOD aside as dead weight.
He's like a tumbleweed on the prairie, out of touch with the good earth.
He lives rootless and aimless in a land where nothing grows."

JEREMIAH 17:5–6 MSG

It's so easy and often natural to depend on those around you. Truth is, you probably have some amazing people in your life who are dependable and love you. They want the best for you. They have your back without fail. And when the going gets tough, they are your first line of defense—the ones you call first for help. They may be a gift from God, but they are not your Savior.

The Word says that when we depend on others and set God aside, we'll find ourselves aimless. Our faith won't grow because we're not sowing into it. And depending on others is a dangerous precedent to set. We need to train ourselves to see God as our number one. We need to recognize that Jesus is our Savior. . .*alone*. So ask Him to refocus your heart so no one takes that top spot away.

Father, thank You for the amazing community of people who
surround me. I know they are a blessing from You. But help
me remember that You are the only One who can truly save
me. You're my number one. In Jesus' name I pray. Amen.

Let God Carry Your Load

Pile your troubles on GOD's shoulders—he'll carry your load,
he'll help you out. He'll never let good people topple into ruin.

PSALM 55:22 MSG

The weight of worry is a heavy load to carry. The stress can feel almost unbearable to lug around from day to day. And when you add fear into the mix, your knees begin to buckle under the burden. We may be good at multitasking and have strength forged by fire, but we're not Wonder Woman. We're not Super Girl. And given enough time, we will be crushed.

Thank the Lord that He offers to carry our load for us. Will you trust Him with it? Spend time today unpacking every burden weighing heavily on your shoulders. Don't leave out any detail, no matter how small. Feel it lift minute by minute. Take in deep breaths and exhale as you destress. Have faith God will take the load off you and replace it with His peace. Believe He will bring healing to your heart. And trust the Lord to set you on the path of freedom.

Father, I'm so thankful for You. Sometimes Your kindness is overwhelming and I feel unworthy of it. But I'm going to take You up on Your generous offer and offload my worries in exchange for Your peace. And when I forget, nudge me to remember. I know I can trust You with it all! In Jesus' name I pray. Amen.

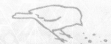

When Your World Blows Up

God is our refuge and strength, a tested help in times of trouble. And so
we need not fear even if the world blows up and the mountains crumble
into the sea. Let the oceans roar and foam; let the mountains tremble!

PSALM 46:1–3 TLB

Sometimes life feels like a series of explosions. Without warning, things around us implode. A marriage blows up. A friendship crumbles. Our savings is depleted. Our heart breaks. A disease appears. A parent dies. Another pregnancy test is negative. And we feel helpless. That's when we need to let our faith rise up as we cry out for God to strengthen and save.

With the craziness of the world on display more and more every day, let this verse fill you with a sense of calm. Allow the reminder that God is your refuge and strength to settle your spirit. Let it refocus your faith and rework your perspective. It has the power to pull you from the pit of hopelessness because it releases you from being in control. Now more than ever, we need to remember that nothing is bigger than God.

Father, this has been a tough season. I can hardly believe
the number of explosions I've had to deal with recently.
Will they ever stop? Will I ever recover? Please be my refuge
and strength. Be the One who brings peace to my weary
heart. Be the One who comforts me. I need help to navigate
the land mines in my life. In Jesus' name I pray. Amen.

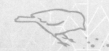

The Power of Discernment

*The one with a wise heart is called "discerning," and speaking
sweetly to others makes your teaching even more convincing.*

PROVERBS 16:21 TPT

Some of us are born with wisdom. We have an innate sense of right and
wrong. But if you don't have natural discernment, don't hesitate to ask
God for it. It's a gift He freely gives, and it's vital for living a faith-filled
life that glorifies the Lord because it helps you choose well. It opens your
eyes to underlying issues and helps you distinguish good from evil. Since
the answers you're looking for aren't always cut and dried, sometimes
you'll struggle to know what's best in a certain situation. That's why a
discerning spirit is so important.

Even more, consider that those around you take note of your life.
If they know you're a Jesus girl, they look at how you live. They watch
how you act and what you say. They scrutinize the decisions you make.
They notice your choices and how they line up with what you preach.
So having discernment not only is valuable for you but has far-reaching
effects through the power of your testimony too.

Father, fill me with discernment. Let Your Holy Spirit in
me guide my decisions. Mature my faith so I understand the
importance of a discerning heart, and help me steward it well.
Make me ever aware of my testimony so my choices encourage
others to seek Your face. In Jesus' name I pray. Amen.

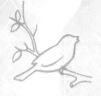

It's Not Up to You

He came to save us. It's not that we earned it by doing good works
or righteous deeds; He came because He is merciful. He brought us out
of our old ways of living to a new beginning through the washing of
regeneration; and He made us completely new through the Holy Spirit,
who was poured out in abundance through Jesus the Anointed, our Savior.

TITUS 3:5–6 VOICE

What a relief to know we aren't responsible for earning eternal life with
God. Think about it, friend! Remember all those poor choices you made
as a teenager? Remember the times you broke the rules or broke the law?
Think about the compromises you made morally. Think about situations
where your words and actions didn't line up with God's will and ways.
If salvation were up to us, we'd be in huge trouble.

But our amazing Father sent His one and only Son to save us. God
knew we could never be the answer. Our sinfulness would always be a
barrier. So in His mercy, Jesus shed His blood on the cross and washed us
clean. He paid the price we could never pay ourselves. And it's our faith
in Christ—who He is and what He has done—that opens the door to
heaven for us. Through our belief in Him, we are made new!

Father, my salvation is because of Your Son.
I'm humbled and grateful. Thank You for not
leaving it up to me. In Jesus' name I pray. Amen.

Waiting in Silence for God

My soul, wait silently for God alone, for my expectation is
from Him. He only is my rock and my salvation; He is my
defense; I shall not be moved. In God is my salvation and my
glory; the rock of my strength, and my refuge, is in God.

PSALM 62:5–7 NKJV

What does it mean to wait silently for God alone? Maybe it's a reminder to refrain from talking to anyone who will listen. Sometimes we just want to chew on our situation with others, amen? We want opinions. We want to dissect. We want to look at it from every angle. We're excellent at ruminating about what's on our heart.

But there's something powerful about silence. It carries weight. Rather than asking the advice of others, we stay quiet as we wait to hear from God. We give Him dibs on what insight we subscribe to. Waiting silently for God alone means recognizing His authority above all else. It's acknowledging the significance He holds in our life. It's allowing our faith to rise up to the heavens as we wait for His voice to break the silence.

Father, help me know when to unpack my heart with others and when to wait on You. I want to honor who You are in my life and the authority You carry. Let me find comfort knowing You're my rock, my defense, my strength, and my refuge. In Jesus' name I pray. Amen.

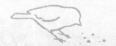

God Never Changes

Jesus the Anointed One is always the same: yesterday, today, and forever.
HEBREWS 13:8 VOICE

The truth that God never changes is epic news for the believer, especially because the world changes all the time. It's not only clothing trends and hairstyles that cycle, but also what society sees as right and wrong. And if we were to be honest, we'd admit some of the changes we're witnessing in our nation and world are destabilizing. That's why it's so important we cling to the truth that God doesn't change.

God cannot be swayed by persuasive arguments. He never compromises. He doesn't bend the rules. And His promises from thousands of years ago still stand true today. Friend, hold on to this bit of awesomeness when you start feeling worried or scared. God will always rescue. He'll restore and bring peace, meeting every need you have. And every time you cry out, your voice will reach His ears. Keep the faith even when everything around you seems to be crumbling, because God will always piece you back together.

Father, it's hard to stay focused and faithful because of
the decline I'm seeing in the world today. Honestly, I'm
afraid of all the changes and what they might mean for me
and those I love. What a relief to know You don't change!
I can cling to You for stability and security. And that
makes all the difference! In Jesus' name I pray. Amen.

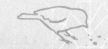

God Is Always Faithful

*Every promise from the faithful God is pure and
proves to be true. He is a wraparound shield of
protection for all his lovers who run to hide in him.*

PROVERBS 30:5 TPT

It's hard to know who to trust these days with all the fake news and
biased reporting across the board. Where we used to subscribe to those
voices we considered to be voices of truth, these days we just don't know.
We're led to believe that what we're hearing is true, but then we learn
it's not even close. We're left feeling confused and frustrated because we
just want someone to level with us. Amen?

Well, friend, you can always count on God as a trustworthy source.
He is incapable of lying or breaking promises. That means you never
have to worry if what the Word says is real. You don't have to question
God's motives or worry He may change His mind. Instead, your faith
will settle your anxious heart and bring comfort from His truths. As a
matter of fact, His words will wrap you up in supernatural peace. God
promises to protect you when you tuck away with Him. So let your faith
rise up as you run into His arms.

> Father, knowing who to believe and trust can be
> confusing. But there's no guessing with You. I can
> always trust You, Your words, and Your promises
> no matter what. In Jesus' name I pray. Amen.

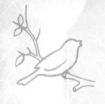

You Need His Help

Help me to do your will, for you are my God.
Lead me in good paths, for your Spirit is good.

PSALM 143:10 TLB

When God asks something of us, He will help us walk it out. In our excitement, we might take off running toward the finish line and forget to rely on the Lord for what we need. We work in our own strength, cling to our own wisdom, and focus on our own ways. But in the end, we crash and burn. The reality is that what God asks of us requires His help. We simply can't do it without Him.

Is God asking you to start a ministry? Lead a small group? Start an outreach in your community? Write a book? Share your testimony from the stage? Raise a special needs child? Change your career focus? Move to a different country for mission work? Free up financial resources? Whatever God is asking you to do comes with His toolkit. Friend, you will need His help. Have faith in the Lord to reveal every next step and equip you with the courage and confidence to follow His lead. You've been invited into an adventure, and God will be the One to guide you through it.

Father, thank You for trusting me to do Your work. What an honor and privilege to be Your hands and feet! Lead me and equip me as I follow You. In Jesus' name I pray. Amen.

What Would Make You Satisfied?

Empty out of my heart everything that is false—every lie, and every crooked thing. And give me neither undue poverty nor undue wealth—but rather, feed my soul with the measure of prosperity that pleases you. May my satisfaction be found in you. Don't let me be so rich that I don't need you or so poor that I have to resort to dishonesty just to make ends meet. Then my life will never detract from bringing glory to your name.

PROVERBS 30:8–9 TPT

What would it look like for you to be satisfied? What would allow you to stay in a place of contentment so you weren't worried about your welfare nor convinced God's help was unnecessary? Take time today to journal about your response to this question. There's a fine line between having too little and having too much, so invite the Lord to help you map this out. Ask Him to remove preconceived ideas or worldly ideals. And think about what earthly and spiritual needs would allow for your satisfaction to be found solely in God.

The writer of today's scripture passage shows great wisdom, realizing too much or too little might work against him. His goal is bringing glory to God's name with his life, and ours should be too. This is an exercise in faith, friend. There's no right or wrong. Instead, let it open your eyes to your level of trust in God's provision.

Father, show me how to be satisfied in You. In Jesus' name I pray. Amen.

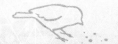

173

The Path of Faith

*Before every person there is a path that seems like
the right one to take, but it leads straight to hell!*

PROVERBS 16:25 TPT

How many times have you chosen the path you thought was right, but it ended up being very wrong? You saw the warning flags and ignored them. Maybe you decided you were too deeply committed to back out, even though you had a gut check that made you think differently. When you're that far in, changing course can be difficult. And often at the end of these paths are difficult consequences to walk out.

Settle in your heart that Jesus is the only way to eternal life. There is only one path, and it's through Him. Alone. The world may tell you all roads lead to God. Or they'll say there are several paths to choose from. Others may try to convince you there is no life after death. But let your faith rise up with unflinching belief in Jesus Christ and in the salvation purchased by His death on the cross. It's important you receive the gift of salvation now so you can spend eternity in the presence of God.

Father, today I am reaffirming my faith in Your Son, Jesus.
I believe His complete work on the cross paid the price for
my sins. Give me the courage and confidence to walk that
path of faith every day! In Jesus' name I pray. Amen.

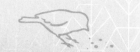

Be a Light

There is a generation rising that is so filled with pride,
they think they are superior and look down on others. There
is a generation rising that uses their words like swords to cut
and slash those who are different. They would devour the poor,
the needy, and the afflicted from off the face of the earth!

PROVERBS 30:13–14 TPT

Because the Bible is alive and active and always relevant, we can see this decline is still so true today. It seems as if each generation moves the dial a little more toward evil, and the fallout can leave us feeling hopeless. But God doesn't feel that way. He is the One to lift our head and infuse our weary spirit with hope and peace. And even when things look dark, He will help us be a source of light.

Decide to be a strong woman of faith who leaves others better than before. Speak encouragement, choosing to be kind even in hard conversations. Remember that you're no better than anyone else, and refrain from thinking of yourself as superior in any way. Watch the words that spew from hurt or frustration. There are plenty of unkind people in the world today—don't be one of them.

Father, let me be a light in a world that can be so dark. Let my words and actions bless others as they glorify You. Help my faith rise up to every occasion. In Jesus' name I pray. Amen.

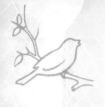

Trusting Others Is
an Empty Hope

*Give us a father's help when we face our enemies. For to trust
in any man is an empty hope. With God's help we will fight
like heroes, and he will trample down our every foe!*

PSALM 60:11–12 TPT

Chances are you have some amazing people in your life who love and support you. They probably abound with encouragement and wisdom and help you figure out life. Maybe they are your mentors. Maybe they are friends and family who have promised to stand in the gap for you. And while they are a blessing in your life in many ways, be careful they don't hold a spot higher than God.

God's Word says that trusting in any man (or woman) is an empty hope. It's a pretty bold statement, but take heed. It's not a slam against your community but rather a reminder that they are imperfect. Even their best intentions will fall short at times. But with God's help, you will find victory. So anchor your faith in Him alone, believing He will help you stand tall in confidence to face what's ahead.

Father, what a great reminder that to place my faith in
those who love me isn't fair to me or them. Or You. I can
appreciate their support and encouragement without
expecting them to be my savior. That role has already
been filled by Your Son. Remind me that You will always
be the hero in my story. In Jesus' name I pray. Amen.

Why You Can Have Bold Confidence

We live in the bold confidence that God hears our voices when we ask for things that fit His plan. And if we have no doubt that He hears our voices, we can be assured that He moves in response to our call.

1 JOHN 5:14–15 VOICE

Do you have bold confidence God hears you? That's a big statement of faith many may not be able to claim. We might think He hears us some of the time. We might decide our prayers break through the ceiling most of the time, especially when we're praying something of interest. Or we may feel our repeat requests have worn God out. But what would it look like not only to have bold confidence that God hears the prayers that align with His plan, but also to trust He'll answer every one of them?

It would look like standing strong when the storms hit because you know God is working in them. It's feeling relieved rather than stressed out because you chose to surrender to His plan. It's living in peace and not fear because you took what worried you straight to God. Your faith is a fast pass to bold confidence. Let it rise up with unshakable belief that you are heard and that He will answer.

Father, help me settle in my heart that You want
to hear from me because You care about what
I care about. In Jesus' name I pray. Amen.

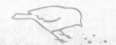

177

Reminding Ourselves

Keep up your reputation, God—give me life! In your justice, get me out
of this trouble! In your great love, vanquish my enemies; make a clean
sweep of those who harass me. And why? Because I'm your servant.

PSALM 143:11–12 MSG

What a clever comment from the psalmist. He's telling the Lord to exact
His justice and deliver him from trouble. He's asking God to conquer
the enemy and wipe out those badgering and bullying him. Then he
assures God he's fully and willingly surrendered to Him. But notice he
pleads with the Lord to listen and act because He has a reputation to
keep. This isn't manipulation. It's a man recognizing God's power and
might and reminding Him of a perfect opportunity to bring glory to
His name.

Do you ever remind God of who He is or what He's done? Of course,
such reminders are not for Him but for you. We need to remember all
the times He has come through. We need to recall Bible characters who
saw the mighty hand of God move. Thinking about God's promises is
a wonderful faith-builder. The next time you need help, point back to
a time He intervened—whether in your life or someone else's. Since a
precedence has been set, it means He can do it again.

> Father, thanks for revealing Your power for others to
> see. I'm grateful we can refer back to those times and
> ask for Your help again. In Jesus' name I pray. Amen.

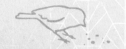

You Belong to God

We all know that everyone fathered by God will not make sin a way of life because God protects His children from the evil one, and the evil one can't touch them. Have confidence in the fact that we belong to God, but also know that the world around us is in the grips of the evil one.

1 JOHN 5:18–19 VOICE

As humans, we walk a line between good and evil. No one is immune to the temptation to walk on the dark side. We all can be swayed to pursue what the flesh wants over what we may know to be true. Even when we clearly see the wrong way, sometimes we choose it anyway. But when we place our faith in the Lord and purpose to live a righteous life, we're protected from the enemy. As God's children, we can trust Him to keep us from willfully walking that sinful path as a way of life.

Be confident of this truth: you're supernaturally protected by your Father. That doesn't mean you won't mess up or have seasons of sinning. And it doesn't mean you won't be tempted to make the wrong choices. But while the world around you may be in the enemy's grip, you won't be. Instead, your faith says you belong to God. And He's a protective parent indeed.

> Father, thank You for protecting me from the
> enemy and keeping me from embracing evil
> as a way of life. In Jesus' name I pray. Amen.

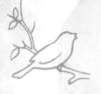

Warrior or Wait-er?

Do you want to be a mighty warrior? It's better to be known as one who is patient and slow to anger. Do you want to conquer a city? Rule over your temper before you attempt to rule a city.

PROVERBS 16:32 TPT

Many of us want to be known as warriors. We want that tough-girl reputation because it makes us feel strong. It makes us feel capable. It helps us find the courage to work through the mess ahead and the confidence to keep going when the going gets tough. And honestly, there are days we need to feel like we're in control because everything around us feels chaotic.

But notice that God puts a premium on being patient and slow to anger. Why? Because sometimes we need to take a step back to take in the situation. Rather than coming out of the corner with claws bared, managing our response reveals a level of maturity. Keeping our temper in check gives God time to speak into our heart and offer perspective. So lean into your faith and let it be your guide when you're faced with a choice of responses. Ask God to show you what to do next.

Father, being someone who waits is a real challenge! So often my response is to rise up in warrior mode rather than in faith. I let my flesh win out. Teach me to be patient and slow to anger. I definitely need Your help. In Jesus' name I pray. Amen.

They Can't, but God Can

Don't put your life in the hands of experts who know
nothing of life, of salvation life. Mere humans don't have
what it takes; when they die, their projects die with them.
PSALM 146:3–4 MSG

God reminds us often throughout His Word not to put our trust in humankind. But knowing He created us to live and thrive in community, why is this message so important for us to hear repeatedly? Maybe it's because our normal response to life's difficulties is to circle the wagons and try to figure out things together.

Think about it. We crave being able to touch and see each other when we're worried. We like reassuring hugs and caring smiles. We like having someone next to us while we're getting the doctor's report or sitting in court. We want others to physically be with us so we can verbally process the situation. But we get into trouble when we decide they're the ones to save us. . .not God. Other people can't offer salvation. They can't bring supernatural peace. They can't heal our hearts in the way we need. Love those who love you, but put your faith in the only One who saves.

> Father, keep my eyes focused on You for the kind
> of help and healing that requires Your hand. I'm
> grateful for the people You've put in my life, but my
> hope is in You alone. In Jesus' name I pray. Amen.

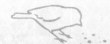

The Waters, Rivers, and Fires of Life

When you go through deep waters and great trouble, I will be with you. When you go through rivers of difficulty, you will not drown! When you walk through the fire of oppression, you will not be burned up—the flames will not consume you.

Isaiah 43:2 TLB

No matter what life throws your way, your faith in God is what makes these terrible seasons bearable. Trusting Him to strengthen you will carry you through each trial and tribulation safely. And pressing into Him for help will allow you to come out the other side intact. We need God to be near to us because sometimes life is just too big and overwhelming to handle without Him.

What deep waters, rivers of difficulty, or fires of oppression are you facing today? Did the adoption process fall through? Did you find inappropriate text messages from your husband to another? Did you suffer through a natural disaster? Is your loneliness palpable? Did you lose a parent? Are you feeling hopeless financially? Friend, activate your faith and run to God. He sees you and will be with you through it all. Let Him restore what has been lost.

> Father, I desperately need You right now. I'm in so deep and can't see a way forward. You know everything I'm feeling and the details of my struggles, and I'm asking You to help me get through them. In Jesus' name I pray. Amen.

When You Crave a Brand-New Thing

For I'm going to do a brand-new thing. See, I have already begun!
Don't you see it? I will make a road through the wilderness of the world
for my people to go home, and create rivers for them in the desert!

ISAIAH 43:19 TLB

Sometimes we're just ready for a change. We want a fresh take on life because ours feels stale. We're ready for something new to shake up old ways and old habits. Maybe your marriage feels stagnant. Maybe the daily routine with the kids feels humdrum. Maybe your quiet time with God feels flat. Maybe your work attitude or environment has soured. These are normal responses we all have from time to time.

How wonderful to serve a God who is up for rejuvenation! His specialty is transformation. He is the source of revival, and He's ready to do brand-new things in your life. When asked, God will carve out new roads through the lonely and monotonous wilderness to new lands. Yes, you can have the reinvigoration you're craving in life when you put your faith in Him. Life with God is an adventure, full of rebirth and renewal. It may not always be easy, but it will always be worth it.

> Father, I'm ready for a brand-new thing. I need to be
> revitalized to get excitement back for certain things
> in my life. Let's do this! In Jesus' name I pray. Amen.

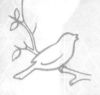

Following the Lord

I hear the Lord saying, "I will stay close to you, instructing and guiding you along the pathway for your life. I will advise you along the way and lead you forth with my eyes as your guide. So don't make it difficult; don't be stubborn when I take you where you've not been before. Don't make me tug you and pull you along. Just come with me!"

PSALM 32:8–9 TPT

Many who are committed to God talk about following the Lord as if it's a simple process. We want to glorify Him with our life, but it's anything but easy. If you've tried, you understand. Can we just admit that following God is much easier said than done?

That's why today's verse is so important. It's from the Lord's point of view, and chances are we can all relate. As we choose to follow God, He promises to stick close by and guide us. He offers insight, scouting out what's ahead. But God also knows we'll probably buck the plans He has in place. He understands that our prideful heart makes us stubborn at times. And He also knows there are moments when we must be lovingly prodded along because of fear or insecurity. When we activate our faith and remember God knows what's best, we'll find the peace we need to surrender to the One who always has our best interests in mind.

Father, help me follow Your lead.
Always. In Jesus' name I pray. Amen.

When You Face Abandonment

So don't turn your face away from me. You're the God of my salvation; how can you reject your servant in anger? You've been my only hope, so don't forsake me now when I need you! My father and mother abandoned me. But you, Yahweh, took me in and made me yours.

PSALM 27:9–10 TPT

We've all felt the sting of abandonment by those we never thought would leave. Marriages have blown up. Friends have walked away. Families have splintered. It's a painful reality everyone can relate to. But there are some whose own parents have walked away—a rejection causing unmatched heartache.

No matter what your earthly mom or dad was like, you will always have a perfect heavenly Father whose love will never change. The truth is, nothing you can do will ever increase or diminish God's love for you. Nothing you do or say will make Him reject or abandon you. Through faith, you are His forever and always.

Father, I know the pain of rejection and abandonment.
Sometimes certain people and situations trigger memories
of how it made me feel. Please heal me from that hurt,
Lord, and speak value into my weary heart. Remind me
I am loved. Remind me I am significant. And fill me with
confidence in Your love. In Jesus' name I pray. Amen.

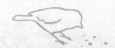

The Endgame of Eternity

One thing I have desired of the LORD, that will I seek: that I may dwell in the house of the LORD all the days of my life, to behold the beauty of the LORD, and to inquire in His temple. For in the time of trouble He shall hide me in His pavilion; in the secret place of His tabernacle He shall hide me; He shall set me high upon a rock.

PSALM 27:4–5 NKJV

Dwelling in God's house forever—this should be the desire of every follower of Jesus! The endgame is eternity with God in heaven, which means this life is not your final destination. Don't get too connected to the here and now. Instead, keep your eyes fixed on God. He will keep your heart focused on what is true and right. Remember that what this world offers will pale in comparison to the glory you'll see in heaven. There will be no words to describe it.

Friend, this life of faith you are walking out is but a breath. Spend it sharing the Good News with those around you. Be the hands and feet of Jesus whenever possible. Encourage those who are struggling with the truth of God's Word. Grow your relationship with the Lord, letting Him be your true north. And in all situations, let your faith rise up to meet every challenge that comes your way.

Father, today and forever. . .I'm all in.
In Jesus' name I pray. Amen.

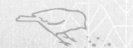

Scripture Index

More Inspiration for Your Beautiful Soul

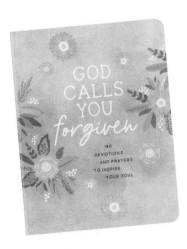
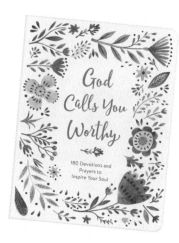

These delightful devotionals—created just for you—will encourage and inspire your soul with deeply rooted truths from God's Word. Each devotional reading will assure you that God's Word is unchanging and will help you to grow in your faith as you become the beautifully courageous woman the heavenly Creator intended you to be!

Flexible Casebound / $12.99 each

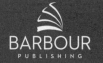